William Greaves was born in Pontefract, West Yorkshire, and after periods on local weekly and regional evening newspapers joined the *Daily Mail* in Manchester as a news reporter in time to chronicle the arrival of The Beatles and the Mersey Sound to Liverpool in the Swinging Sixties.

Summoned to Fleet Street, he soon revealed a flair for the unusual, arcane and amusing story and became the daily author of the *Mail*'s then-famous front page End Column for several years before being elevated to feature writer.

Since leaving the *Mail* to become a freelance, he has been variously columnist, feature writer and television critic with the *Today* newspaper, *The Times*, the *Daily Telegraph* and *Radio Times*.

A life-long cricket enthusiast, he is still president of the *Daily Mail* Cricket Club and is founder and trustee of the charity Capital Kids Cricket, which has succeeded in restoring the teaching of the game to nearly a thousand primary and secondary state schools in inner London.

As a 'menopausal diversion' from journalism, he also owned and occasionally ran the *Queen's Head* in Chesham, Buckinghamshire, for five years during the late 1970s, discovering in the process that all adult males know two jobs – their own and how to run a pub... Until they try it.

Married to fellow journalist Suzanne Greaves, he has three children and lives in Islington, north London.

IT'S MY ROUND

A personal celebration of
2,000 years of the British Pub

By William Greaves

Revel Barker Publishing

First published by Revel Barker Publishing in 2011

ISBN: 978-1-907841-07-1

Revel Barker Publishing
66 Florence Road, Brighton, England BN1 6DJ
revelbarker@gmail.com

To Suzanne, who has devotedly shared all the amazingly happy interludes between newspaper assignments and the summons of pub or cricket field.

Contents

Between rounds... How the pub used to take to the rails. Recalling the great days of the real buffet car.

CHAPTER SIXTEEN
Since records began
The oldest, the smallest, the highest, the lowest and a few other record holders.
Between rounds... Beer or ale? – the brew through the ages.

CHAPTER SEVENTEEN
Smuggling up
The pubs that once relied on keeping their eyes open – and their mouths shut.

CHAPTER EIGHTEEN
Keeping it in the family – and keeping the whole thing going
The way they used to be – and maybe should consider staying.

Chapter one

The call of the pelican

For a lifelong devotee of the British Pub it was indeed a defining moment.

OK, so it was 11 in the morning. Even devotees of British pubs don't usually start boozing at 11 in the morning. But back home in London, on the other side of the world, it was 4am. And 4am in London was my personal clocking-off time.

The very last tickles to the front page had been well and truly tickled and for an ageing scribbler on assignment in Hong Kong it was time to enjoy a few hours' well-earned sleep.

As weary footsteps made their way back to featureless international hotel, the sign on the building on the pavement alongside shone like a beacon of hope in the late morning sunshine. *The Pickled Pelican*. Oh, my word! And on special offer – Tetley's Bitter on draught. In the corner of what could almost be described as a snug, BBC TV offered Auntie's latest news in reassuringly Queen-like English. And the sign on the wall bore the kind of idiotic philosophy regularly imparted to the drinking classes: BEER IS THE ANSWER – BUT CAN ANYONE REMEMBER THE QUESTION?

This was new China, complete with towering skyscrapers, neon lights, strange hieroglyphics, strangulated vowels and scurrying feet, but what self-respecting Brit could pass by an establishment that called itself *The Pickled Pelican*?

In truth, I've never heard of a British pub called *The Pickled Pelican*. But who can deny that The Pickled Pelican *sounds* like a British pub? I mean, it doesn't suggest a delicatessen, does it? Or even a fish and chippie. Or a pet shop. It sounds like a boozer.

So there I was, ensconced in the news pages of the *South China Morning Post* with foaming pint in hand, when an unexpected voice interrupted my desultory researches.

'Do you know, Bill, I might join you in one of those.'

Looking up, I found myself face to familiar face with ace newshound and enthusiastic amateur wicketkeeper, Nick Bryant, the BBC's man in Australia and former *Daily Mail* colleague in London, who just happened to be *en route* with new wife, Fleur, from their wedding in Sri Lanka to his home in Sydney.

Unexpectedly astray in a foreign land, he, too, had found the call of *The Pickled Pelican* irresistible and in no time we were catching up on each other's life and times.

It took several more pints – served in proper dimpled glasses, needless to say, complete with handles – to carry out this exchange of information for the simple reason that we had not clapped eyes on each other these past fourteen years.

All of which goes to prove, if any such proof be necessary, that the British pub is unique. It flutters its come-hither eyelids and the faithful, wherever they find themselves, come running to its bosom.

Like this particular hostelry, attempts to recreate it have been made all over the world.

Nostalgic expats, homesick tourists and workers on international errand – myself included – have sought comfort in the *Queen Victoria* in Florence, the *Duke of Wellington* in Beirut, the *Britannia* in Monte Carlo, the *Crown* in Cusco, Peru, the *Cock Tavern* in Las Palmas, the *British Grenadier* in Vienna, the *Winston Churchill* in Paris, the *Old Bell* in Amsterdam, the *Red Lion* in Bimini, Bahamas, the *Lord's Pub*, would you believe, in Garmisch-Partenkirchen, Bavaria, Germany – even *The Pub*, plain and simple, in Valletta, Malta.

And when Martyn Terpilowski, a 34-year-old investment broker from Barrow-in-Furness, received an offer from his boss to pay for a flight out of Tokyo after the tsunami disaster and subsequent nuclear radiation crisis of March, 2011, his first response was to consider the matter over a couple of pints of Guinness at the *Mermaid* pub in that city – which, according to the *Daily Telegraph*'s

Nick Allen, is 'a cosy, sticky-floored boozer that looks like it has been transplanted from the City of London.'

But these establishments remain today what they always were, incongruous idiosyncrasies in a foreign field, frequented only by Brits on their travels – such as Nick Bryant and myself – and the odd native anglophile.

So before we embark upon a personal tribute to a priceless national institution, perhaps we should define the nature of the beast. What exactly are the ingredients that distinguish the British Pub from all those other oases of refreshment throughout the rest of the thirsty world?

One obvious difference is the very one so spectacularly exemplified by that chance meeting with an old buddy. Unlike bars and other mere drinking places, pubs are not where folk arrange to meet but places where the like-minded happen to congregate, like Mallory and Irving on Mount Everest all those years ago, for no better reason than *because they are there*.

As with church or bus-stop, the pub summons to its presence those who know instinctively when and where to assemble. No phone calls, no emails – just an irresistible magnetic force that grabs the faithful by the scruff of the neck and marches their unresisting footsteps towards an immediate and predetermined destiny.

But other differences are equally significant.

First and foremost, the pub is someone's home. It is a haven of welcome, occupied by a resident landlord – respectfully acknow-ledged to be the guv'nor – or landlady or, more often, both, whose generous predisposition is to preside over an asylum for friends, neighbours and passers-by. It is not a bar – it is a public *house*.

Back where it really belongs, in a British village, town or city as opposed to Hong Kong, Sidi Barrani or wherever, the pub makes no attempt to advertise its *raison d'être*. If folk don't know what they are looking for or how to recognise it when they stumble across it, they must expect to remain unfulfilled.

Its name offers no clue – a bit of regal anatomy, perhaps, like *Queen's Head* or *King's Arms*, whole menageries of the animal kingdom such as *Hare and Hounds*, *Golden Bear*, *Dog & Duck*, *Black*

Bull or *Red Lion* or perhaps some local sporting activity like *The Cricketers* or *The Anglers' Rest* seldom means to imply that king, queen, hare, hound, bear, bull, lion or men in white flannels or chest waders are awaiting inside to greet the visitor, although friendly dogs – but seldom ducks – may lurk beneath tables, munching their way through packets of cheese and onion crisps.

Nor do its street windows give anything away. However large, they are usually constructed of opaque glass or, in the case of many rustic establishments, bottle glass full of circular swirls. Either way, they totally obscure the nature and the occupants of the rooms within. The fact that you are enjoying a few pints with your chums does not require you to be visible to spouse, employer, parents, children, lover or the law.

By far the most significant characteristics of the British Pub, however, are social and historical rather than structural.

For example, unlike clubs, societies or often even churches, pub patrons are not collected together by colour, creed, language, job description, wealth or stature. When first arriving in a new neighbourhood, the very act of walking into 'the local' un-equivocally disassociates the customer from any such prejudices. Pubs, by definition, are for the public, in all its shapes and forms.

THE ALMA (A good friend, retired High Court judge and clan chieftain, now resident in the Scottish highlands, never fails to visit one of his favourite north London pub haunts whenever he returns to the metropolis – *The Alma* in Newington Green. Once there he is surrounded by familiar folk, some of whom he defended as a barrister before his elevation and others he has subsequently been obliged to send down for periods of custodial reflection. He is seldom allowed to put his hand in his pocket. He is back among friends.)

True, there are 'posh' pubs and 'rough' pubs but these are only representative of the location and the social standing of the predominant population thereabouts. Any 'posh' pub that refuses to serve a customer in donkey jacket and working trousers (save politely asking for muddy shoes to be left outside) and any 'rough' pub that shuns the patronage of a chap in dinner suit and lady in gown and elbow-length gloves would not qualify to call itself a pub in the first place. (Posh and rough pubs exist only in urban areas anyway – out in the country the loftiest landowner and humblest serf have long since learnt to depend on each other's allegiance, both commercially and socially.)

Nor is the pub primarily a place to drink. Bars and hotels serve drink; pubs serve a need for companionship. Pubs can't be built – they are a way of life.

What they do provide is the social equivalent of the parish notice board, with additional information that would never have passed the vicar's censorious blue pencil, together with every local service ranging from job centre, through market stall to small ads column. Regulars who set out for a pint or two and return home with five pounds of King Edwards or a couple of fresh-caught mackerel do so because five pounds of King Edwards or a couple of mackerel happen to be what someone else came in with.

On the other hand, pub regulars expected to return home armed with Agatha Jones' wedding date, for example, or the weight of Belinda's baby or the time and place of the next car boot sale never fail to disappoint. Such detail seldom springs to light on the pub agenda of acceptable conversation.

Saloon or public bar chat begins with a casually offered snippet – 'So Chalky's gaff was broken into again last night...' and develops along totally haphazard lines, involving many summaries from expert landlord or landlady for the benefit of new arrivals, until Chalky's misfortune has long since been forgotten but everything else worth knowing has been thoroughly aired.

...Because folk do not foregather in the pub by accident or arrangement, at certain times on certain days, or even on certain times of every day, they *belong* there. They are members of that most resolute and irrepressible breed, the pub regular, whose presence at the bar can be safely predicted by other members.

'Not seen Fred for a day or two' is another way of saying 'Is Fred ill?' 'Is Fred dead?' 'Is Fred on holiday?' or 'Is Fred under house arrest?' What it does not mean is 'Has Fred found something else to do?' or 'Is Fred coming in at a different time of day?'

Another essential purpose of the pub is the service it provides to everyone and anyone who wants something done. Pub regulars have no need to explore classified ads, Yellow Pages or the internet to find what skill they seek. Any self-respecting establishment should contain its representative builder, plumber, electrician, plasterer, carpenter, curtain putter-upper, carpet fitter, lawyer, vicar, undertaker, computer wizard, butcher, dog groomer, gynaecologist, someone who can spell gynaecologist, French-speaker, citizen's advice official and skilled letter writer. Surreptitious suppliers of adult toys or cheap fags are a bonus and an insider from the local cop shop something of a luxury. If any of these are temporarily missing, there should be someone who knows where he or she can be found.

(Only one occupation is usually lacking from the pub clientele. The village general practitioner is generally advised to drink outside the boundaries of his or her practice for fear of being

bombarded with symptoms by regulars in search of a privately-owned National Health Service.

When living in the small Buckinghamshire township of Chesham, a doctor friend and I would often venture about six miles to *The Two Brewers* in the charming village of Chipperfield on a Sunday evening so that he might enjoy a few uninterrupted pints. Some-times we overdid it. Meeting him in the high street one Monday lunchtime after our night before, I enquired how his morning had gone. 'Terrible,' he said. 'There were 27 people in the surgery and not one of them was as ill as I was…')

But above and beyond all these distinguishing elements lies the one key factor that determines the ultimate point of departure between the British pub and the world's bar – a distinction that lies in a custom whose origins are buried in the dim and distant past.

There is one familiar expression in the English language that appears in no international phrase book – for the simple reason that foreigners would be able to make neither head nor tail of it. The phrase is: 'It's my shout.' It has a number of variations: the assertive 'No, no, it's definitely my shout,' the quizzically aggrieved 'Whose shout is it?' and even the faintly aggressive 'It can't be my shout again, surely?'

The 'shout' is not a shout as in an exclamation, of course. In pub parlance, a shout is an offer to dig deep to slake the thirst of one's companions at one's personal expense.

When two or more people assemble to quench their thirst in a public place anywhere east of Dover or west of the Scillies, a bill is pushed under the saucer each time a new batch of drinks arrives. Or a beer mat is marked, slate chalked or spike spiked. Upon departure, the final tally is then added up and divided among all present. Fair – but unsporting.

No nation that invented cricket could seriously be expected to comply with a code of conduct so morosely bereft of complication that all the niceties of lifemanship and etiquette are swamped by simple arithmetic. So the difference between the British pub and every other kind of alien bar is that, here, we pay before we sip. Correction: one person pays before everyone sips.

So the British pub – and the atmosphere that prevails within – is unique in so much as every new order is a personal gift by one patron to all his or her friends or colleagues.

But who is that one patron? Here is the nub around which the very British game of 'pubbing' revolves. For not only is the 'round' (defined in my Collins Concise as 'a number of drinks bought at one time for a number of people') deeply engrained in the national ethos, it is also deliciously ill-defined in the matter of whose turn it is to dig deep.

There was a time, before bitter gave way to Budweiser, when such a question would never have had to be asked. Tyro drinkers would be so overawed by their surroundings – and the dangers that lurked within – that they would nervously ape their experienced elders. In other words, they would learn by natural instinct when it was their turn to put hand in pocket.

Some years ago, in the days when newspapers lived in Fleet Street and the round often assumed titanic dimensions, I became aware that standards were falling. Appalling laxities like tossing a coin or engaging in a game of spoof in order to determine who should pay were creeping in to replace the proper order of things. Some players even sank to the unpardonable depths of 'round avoidance', arriving late, enjoying several drinks and then, in the nick of time, spotting someone across the room with whom they 'must just grab a word'.

It was not entirely the young students' fault. A new and impetuous generation may well have sprung, improperly dressed, upon the scene – but who can learn when the teachers have forgotten how to teach? In those darkest hours, I realised that The Word had to be spread before a glorious national heritage was allowed to wither on the vine.

The result of this initiative became known throughout the pubs in that street of shame as *Greaves's Rules*. Under their auspices not only were rounds ordered but tribunals commissioned and even sentences passed. Once-respected men today walk shoeless down Oxford Street for having transgressed against them.

It was a fragile claim to eponymous immortality – and certainly not one I sought to patent in documentary form – but the *Daily Telegraph* invited me to publish those same edicts as a reminder that nothing in our history is so sacred that it cannot be forgotten.

Greaves's Rules became immortalised in print. (Arguably the second 'S' in Greaves's is superfluous but the *Telegraph* designer plonked it in so there it must remain.)

If *Greaves's Rules* achieved nothing else they were surely proof positive that the British pub is unique – and its 2,000 year history and legacy overdue for investigation.

This is the aged cutting that still adorns the walls of many pubs in Britain:

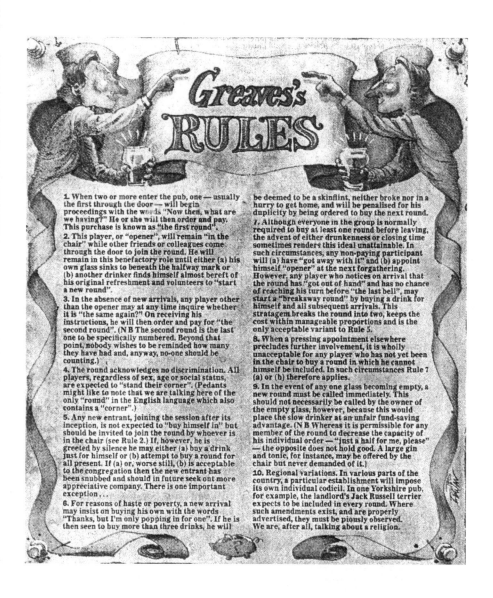

Greaves's RULES

1. When two or more enter the pub, one — usually the first through the door — will begin proceedings with the words "Now then, what are we having?" He or she will then order and pay. This purchase is known as "the first round".

2. This player, or "opener", will remain "in the chair" while other friends or colleagues come through the door to join the round. He will remain in this benefactory role until either (a) his own glass sinks to beneath the halfway mark or (b) another drinker finds himself almost bereft of his original refreshment and volunteers to "start a new round".

3. In the absence of new arrivals, any player other than the opener may at any time inquire whether it is "the same again?" On receiving his instructions, he will then order and pay for "the second round". (N B The second round is the last one to be specifically numbered. Beyond that point, nobody wishes to be reminded how many they have had and, anyway, no-one should be counting.)

4. The round acknowledges no discrimination. All players, regardless of sex, age or social status, are expected to "stand their corner". (Pedants might like to note that we are talking here of the only "round" in the English language which also contains a "corner".)

5. Any new entrant, joining the session after its inception, is not expected to "buy himself in" but should be invited to join the round by whoever is in the chair (see Rule 2.) If, however, he is greeted by silence he may either (a) buy a drink just for himself or (b) attempt to buy a round for all present. If (a) or, worse still, (b) is acceptable to the congregation then the new entrant has been snubbed and should in future seek out more appreciative company. There is one important exception...

6. For reasons of haste or poverty, a new arrival may insist on buying his own with the words "Thanks, but I'm only popping in for one". If he is then seen to buy more than three drinks, he will be deemed to be a skinflint, neither broke nor in a hurry to get home, and will be penalised for his duplicity by being ordered to buy the next round.

7. Although everyone in the group is normally required to buy at least one round before leaving, the advent of either drunkenness or closing time sometimes renders this ideal unattainable. In such circumstances, any non-paying participant will (a) have "got away with it" and (b) appoint himself "opener" at the next forgathering. However, any player who notices on arrival that the round has "got out of hand" and has no chance of reaching his turn before "the last bell", may start a "breakaway round" by buying a drink for himself and all subsequent arrivals. This stratagem breaks the round into two, keeps the cost within manageable proportions and is the only acceptable variant to Rule 5.

8. When a pressing appointment elsewhere precludes further involvement, it is wholly unacceptable for any player who has not yet been in the chair to buy a round in which he cannot himself be included. In such circumstances Rule 7 (a) or (b) therefore applies.

9. In the event of any one glass becoming empty, a new round must be called immediately. This should not necessarily be called by the owner of the empty glass, however, because this would place the slow drinker at an unfair fund-saving advantage. (N B Whereas it is permissible for any member of the round to decrease the capacity of his individual order — "just a half for me, please" — the opposite does not hold good. A large gin and tonic, for instance, may be offered by the chair but never demanded of it.)

10. Regional variations. In various parts of the country, a particular establishment will impose its own individual codicil. In one Yorkshire pub, for example, the landlord's Jack Russell terrier expects to be included in every round. Where such amendments exist, and are properly advertised, they must be piously observed. We are, after all, talking about a religion.

Between rounds...

The first faltering footsteps of *Greaves's Rules* took place one early evening in the early 1970s.

The scene was the editorial floor of the *Daily Mail* newspaper, around which was spread a thirsty bunch of day-shift reporters, eagerly gazing at the clock that would liberate them in the direction of the pub, situated at the bottom of the stairs and just round the corner.

But a crisis had emerged.

There was one in our midst who was fast becoming a proven transgressor of one of the most lamentable crimes in the rule book of drinkers' etiquette.

He stood accused of ducking his round.

It had taken at least twelve months for the evidence to become conclusive. Pub regulars are usually far too determined to 'stand their corner' to notice the existence of a confederate who is not playing the same game. But now the facts were incontrovertible.

If he and one other arrived in the pub at the same time, he would insist it was 'my shout'. Even if there were three, he would demand to be first to foot the bill. In such circumstances, the outlay was deemed to be a sound investment for a lengthy session at others' future expense.

Any greater number than three, however, and the wallet would remain firmly out of view while he enjoyed as many as he dare of fellow drinkers' rounds before making his escape.

Something had to be done about it.

The fateful evening approached. On the pavement outside the public bar of *The Harrow* on Whitefriars Street, just off Fleet Street, there happened to be a men's and ladies' public lavatory, built of sturdy Victorian brickwork and visible as a blur through the opaque window of the bar.

It took ten minutes to orchestrate the structured, surreptitious evacuation of the office, as groups of two or three sidled out and, according to gender, took their place in the appropriate section of the public lavatory.

As soon as the exodus was complete, I suggested to our suspect that it was high time for a 'quick bevy' downstairs.

Predictably, he refused with vehemence my offer to pay for the opening drinks and called up a couple of pints.

A pre-arranged signal through the frosted glass, via a cunningly planted agent who was apparently struggling with an errant umbrella on the pavement, alerted the swelling population of both sections of the public lavatory and between the order and the payment of the opening two drinks, twenty-three cheerful punters arrived through the door in single file to create the biggest one-man round in the chequered history of one of the City of London's most venerated pubs.

It has to be said that our victim responded with remarkably good grace. A round, once embarked upon, had to embrace all new arrivals until superseded by the next order. He paid up half his weekly salary with a wry smile and never misbehaved again.

News of this barrack-room justice spread like wildfire and, almost overnight, created a formula for determining whose turn it was to pay for the next round of drinks, known throughout the murky world of Fleet Street as *Greaves's Rules*.

The only problem was that no one actually knew the rules – least of all their eponymous founder.

Rather more than a decade later, I found myself freshly employed as the freelance television critic of Eddie Shah's new and short-lived daily newspaper, *Today*. In the *Lord High Admiral* pub in Pimlico as the very first editions rolled off the presses, I met up with many of my new colleagues. Most I knew but some only by reputation.

Among the latter was Eric Jacobs, a distinguished former *Sunday Times* man who was now *Today*'s chief features sub editor and Saturday columnist who, like the rest of his colleagues but unlike myself, had been engaged in producing dummy runs for the previous fortnight.

'Are you by chance the Greaves of *Greaves's Rules*?' he enquired when we were introduced. 'Afraid so,' I reluctantly admitted. The bone that he wished to pick immediately became apparent. 'Many times during the last couple of weeks I have attempted to buy a round in this boozer,' he revealed, 'but someone has always chipped in and said: 'No, no, my shout, *Greaves Rules*, old boy...' and far worse was the time when I was attempting to slink off early and some loudmouth once again quoted your damned rules and suggested I put my hand in my pocket.'

The outcome of this confrontation was that the splendid Jacobs bought me lunch and together we hatched up some real rules for the benefit of mankind in general and his next Saturday column in particular.

Thus *Greaves's Rules* made it into print and it was on the strength of that baptism that the *DailyTelegraph* later commissioned me to expand on them under my own byline.

If today they do no more than reinforce the undoubted truth that the British Pub is a law unto itself they will have nobly served their purpose.

Chapter two

Fighting for bitter life

Never since its birth two thousand years ago, as a kind of diplomatic compromise between the Roman invaders' *tabernae* and the *alehouses* already beloved of Boudicca's Ancient Brits, has the very survival of the pub been so finely balanced on the proverbial knife edge.

Here we are in the early years of the twenty-first century and the alarming statistic is that every single week, somewhere in Britain, no fewer than 25 pubs close their doors for the last time. That is to say, 25 more pubs close than new ones open. And that is a net loss of 1,300 a year. (Cheer up – at its worst in 2010 it got up to 39 pubs closing a week. Crisis over?)

There are still an awful lot left but some worthy statistician with nothing better to do – presumably with pint in hand in the *Slug and Lettuce* – recently worked out that, at this rate of closure, last orders would be called for the last time in the last pub in Britain some late evening in June 2037.

So why, after fighting off so many threats over the past two millennia, is the pub suddenly confronted by a vision of Armageddon akin to global warming?

After all, it has survived a succession of invaders – Angles, Saxons, Vikings and Normans – the spread of Christianity, the disapproval of Cromwell's puritans, the challenge of establishments serving such colonial imports as chocolate, coffee and tea and the appearance of the infamous gin palaces of the 18th century to emerge comparatively unscathed by the passage of time.

Indeed, until not that long ago, it used to be the archetypal geography of the British village that it contained on each corner of the central cross roads the 'Four Ps' – Post office, Police station, Parish church and Public house.

In truth, the last village cross roads in England still to boast all four was the otherwise unremarkable community of Great Sankey, on the outskirts of Warrington, in Cheshire, which finally fell off the perch as recently as August, 2004, when, on that occasion, it was not the pub but the post office that gave up the ghost.

And I was there, perched at the bar of the *Chapel House* pub with pint and shorthand notebook in hand, to witness the ultimate demise of a great rustic tradition.

The Rev Michael Buckley was vicar of St Mary's parish church at the time and was no stranger to history. His graveyard, after all, contained the tomb of a Sergeant Donaghue, who blew the bugle that launched the disastrous Charge of the Light Brigade in the Crimean War. 'It's very sad,' he told me, 'but, in a way, it is part of an inevitable sociological process.

'We all have too many outlets for the number of customers. The Church of England is facing up to that fact, pubs are having to diversify in order to survive, the police are concentrating their resources and the Post Office is having to do the same.

'The irony is that the population of Great Sankey was less than a thousand not that long ago and there was more than enough need for all four, and now that it's grown maybe twenty times bigger apparently there isn't.'

Strengthened, doubtless, by the dignity of his office, the reverend gentleman was nonetheless able to allow himself a whimsical smile. 'They reckon the four Ps used to work well together at the hub of the village,' he said. 'The locals could cash their wages at the post office, get drunk at the pub, get arrested at the police station, come over to the church for forgiveness – and then start all over again...'

Holding court in the *Chapel House*, licensee Charlie Morris was more doom-laden. 'It's the end of an era,' he told me. 'I part the curtains in the morning and regularly see half a dozen locals queueing for George to open his post office – even in the pouring rain. It's not just a place for buying stamps, it's a proper post office that does car licences, currency exchange and everything that a village needs.

'But it's not been easy for any of us in recent years. There's been a pub on this site since 1761 – they used to hold inquests and post mortems here – but recently we've twice had to resist bids to turn the site into a McDonalds and a lot of nearby pubs have had to become glorified restaurants.'

Great Sankey's local pub might have survived that particular crisis but the landlord at its epicentre was clearly all too well aware of the storm clouds ahead.

He might, of course, have plucked some courage from the fact that many other crises had been survived over the passing centuries.

For example, way back in the early 13th century, long before parliaments came into being, a burgeoning public clamour to be rid of the scourge of the alehouse led to the emergence of royal decrees to govern what went on within. Curfews were introduced to curb the noisier ones, Canterbury publicans were instructed to serve 'only such as be of good disposition and conversation' and Henry III came up with itinerant inspectors called ale-connors, whose job was to monitor the quality of ale on offer, sometimes commanding mine host either to pour it down the drain, over his own head or – in extreme cases of disapproval – down his own throat!

(Mark you, to be an ale-connor was not always to have the enviable job of being a professional pub crawler. It has been reported that one of their tasks was to don leather breeches and plonk their backsides into a pool of ale for a prescribed period to test it for stickiness – presumably sugar content – although whether greater or less adhesion was deemed to be sought-after perfection has been lost in time.)

Despite many attempts throughout the 14th and 15th centuries to control the downward spiral, such establishments increasingly became hotbeds of loud and ribald revelry until James I, rather unsportingly, found it necessary to decree that 'the purpose of inns, alehouses and victualling-houses' was for 'the receipt, relief and lodging of wayfarers' rather than 'the entertainment of lewd and idle people'.

The lewd and idle had already suffered a setback when in 1495 Henry VII gave local magistrates the power to close alehouses if behaviour within fell below the minimum level of decorum and half a century later Edward VI decreed that would-be alehouse owners had to obtain a licence to open up in the first place. The age of The Licensee had arrived.

Then in the 16th century the explosive fall-out between the oft-married Henry VIII and the Vatican created yet more hurdles along the way. After the Pope's refusal to annul the first marriage of the king to Catherine of Aragon, Henry appointed himself head of a newly-formed Church of England and set about the mass destruction of the Catholic monasteries, which collectively owned about a quarter of Britain's cultivated landscape and an awful lot of its watering holes.

With the disappearance of so many centres of pilgrimage, taverns along the main arterial roads fought for survival and soon were forced publicly to declare their allegiance to the new regime by abandoning former names in favour of a plethora of new-born titles: *Kings Head, Tudor Rose* or anything else they could nick from the royal coat of arms. Even incoming royalist lords of the manor got the kow-tow treatment – the *Earl of Beaconsfield*, the *Bedford Arms*, the *Duke of Buckingham...* the message to all was 'leave us alone, we're on your side'.

Thus the pub lived to fight another day, thereafter comfortably seeing off the discovery of such foreign imports as chocolate, coffee and tea in the mid-17th century.

But the power struggle at monarchy level was to unravel further twists to the plot. On his death in 1685 Charles II left no legitimate heir to the throne – Nell Gwynne's contributions, if any, being ruled out of court – so his brother was invited back from France to become James II. But James' Catholic allegiance left him with few friends among the influential Protestant majority and, although the Duke of Monmouth's revolt was kicked into touch, leading parliamentarians couldn't abide the thought of another string of papal monarchs and invited James's Dutch nephew, William of Orange, over to contest the throne.

William and his army landed in Devon towards the tail end of 1688 and James surrendered sight unseen, handing Mary – his daughter – and husband William a share of the top job. The impact of this succession on the health of the pub was very nearly catastrophic.

Sporting no love for his French neighbours across the Channel, William III's first move was to set up a trade ban that outlawed, among other commodities, an awful lot of wine and every drop of brandy, the latter of which was rapidly gaining favour with the British palate. Smuggling became so rife that William's next response was to encourage the local production of gin.

With all restrictions lifted, the infamous era of the 'gin palace' established itself between 1720 and 1750 with London, in particular, succumbing to a new wave of rowdiness and anti-social behaviour that played into the hands of a growing legion of temperance campaigners. It was estimated that one in every six London dwellings sold alcohol and, despite the nation's historical allegiance to ale, those dispensing gin outnumbered all the capital's inns, taverns and beer-houses put together.

This time, however, it was two developments of the 18th and early 19th centuries that came to the rescue of the foaming pint and its traditional home. With the industrial revolution came the great commercial brewing companies, whose products began to displace the beer brewed by individual licensees, and which increasingly sought to own their own chain of outlets to underpin sales figures and regularise quality. And the brief era of the scheduled stagecoach as the nation's principal personnel and freight carrier created a major expansion of the coaching inn, which quickly re-established itself along a network of main trunk roads to provide food, drink, accommodation and a change of horses for long-distance passengers.

Indeed, by the end of the Victorian era, recovery was complete, local town and village pubs, as well at the roadside inns dotted along the major thoroughfares, proliferated unopposed and few members of the population lived beyond walking distance of their hospitality.

And nor did the greater part of the 20th century – even two world wars and the great depression they bracketed – do anything to weaken the good old British boozer's dominance of all it surveyed.

So why are so many pubs daily calling time for the last time? Can we really be losing our thirst for the survival of a national treasure?

Chapter three

If it ain't broke...

Somewhere back in the mists of time, I was employed as the Ripley district man of the *Derby Evening Telegraph*.

To be honest, Ripley was not the liveliest of towns in those ancient times and little of my sojourn there remains in the memory.

Save one nightly phenomenon.

Ripley pubs closed at 10.30pm whereas the drinkers in nearby Alfreton enjoyed an extra half hour in which to slake their thirst. And casual visitors who knew no better frequently had to leap for the safety of shop entrances as a mighty cavalcade of erratic and bleary-eyed car drivers made their impulsive dash four miles up the road for the couple of extra pints they probably did not need.

Meanwhile, in the North Yorkshire Dales of my childhood and of many scores of nostalgic return visits, there were several pubs in Hawes but only one in Bainbridge – again just four miles away. Hawes drinkers loved to drive to the *Rose and Crown* in Bainbridge for a change and residents of Bainbridge would just as often go in search of a wider choice between *Board Hotel, Crown, Fountain* and *White Hart* in Hawes.

As closing time came round – in this case synchronised at 10.30pm in both cases – the motoring fraternity had two choices of preferred route. Until quite recently the police came to a tacit agreement with the locals – they would patrol the main A684 on one side of the River Ure and leave the minor road on the north bank to sort itself out.

Thus the folk who had seen it through to closing time simultaneously rolled home via the twisty and picturesque alternative route, safe in the knowledge that they were free from prosecution but all too well aware that everyone coming the other way would be just as drunk as they were.

Both the Alfreton stampede and the Wensleydale rat run were equally absurd examples of the dangers of regionally imposed closing times but if, heaven forbid, the British pub really is in its death throes, it could just be that future generations of historians seeking the first manifestation of its demise will look back to the day that Britain finally abandoned the very legislation that most pub regulars loved to hate – licensed hours.

For it is timing that lies at the very heart of pub culture.

Anybody now over the age of 30 began his or her pubbing days in the era of fixed hours of business, when you either got to exactly where you and everyone else knew you were going before 2.30pm or held your thirst in check until 5.30 or 6pm. On Sunday the window of opportunity was restricted even further to a couple of hours between the final blessing of morning Eucharist at 12 noon until 2pm and another three-hour stint between the end of Evensong at 7pm and a good Christian bedtime of 10 o'clock.

It was that wonderfully witty observer of life's frailties and star of countless editions of *Punch* magazine, Basil Boothroyd, who innocently asserted that without licensing hours the great twice-daily ceremony of Opening Time would be lost for ever. 'There would,' he wrote, 'be no sense of anticipation, thrill of delayed delights. You may be able to get a drink whenever you fancy one in those stained old crummy round-the-clock Continental bistros; only here, in the land of the unfree, can we savour the springlike sensation, twice a day, of life beginning anew.' The poor man was blissfully unaware that this daily miracle of re-awakening was doomed to disappear so soon into the slops tray of history.

During the last decades of the twentieth century, Basil's beloved licensing hours were abandoned in favour of all-day opening – largely because visitors from abroad could not understand why they could not pop in for a drink in the middle of the afternoon or why they had to make tracks for bed within ten minutes of the 11pm chimes. These were, of course, the very same visitors who envied and hopelessly tried to copy the institution whose portals, at certain hours, they were barred from entering.

Whatever factions were pressing for all-day opening, it certainly wasn't the overworked pub licensees who were leading the clamour. Nor, I strongly suspect, was it the customers, either.

To keep the place open for at least twelve hours on the trot, landlords and ladies were forced to engage extra bar staff to give them time to put their feet up and keep the books in order and therefore put up the price of drinks to pay for the wages.

Furthermore and far more ominously, regular customers, used to meeting for a 'lunchtime quickie', 'early doors' or 'last knockings' no longer knew when their cronies would be reporting for duty. Drinking by appointment began to rear its ugly head.

After plucking up courage to do away with licensed hours, the politicians were so stunned by their own temerity that they looked wildly about them for any other meddling they could get away with.

It was the start of a positive stampede of 'repairs' to an institution that wasn't broken in the first place.

By well-intentioned ignorance rather than malicious intent, modern-day legislators have done more to endanger the future of the Great British Pub, which publicly they recognise as a priceless asset to the infrastructure of our nation, than any of the puritan regimes of the last two millennia.

The next pressure group to get its way was the 'why should I be stuck at home with the kids while you're in the pub boozing yourself silly?' brigade. All over the land taverns were coerced into agreeing, again by the official demand of the powers-that-be, to open their doors to 'well-behaved children' – despite the fact that many of their customers believed that there was no such animal as a well-behaved child and that they had only ventured out in the first place to get away from their *own* children and certainly had no wish to be surrounded by those belonging to other people.

With the advent of a new 'family' clientele came inevitably the demand for 'something decent to eat'. The selection of pickled and scotch eggs, pickled onions, crisps, gherkins, the odd meat pie and the occasional sandwich that had satisfactorily augmented the serious business of drinking and chatting for generations of customers was no longer deemed to be sufficient.

(There is a pub in deepest Surrey called *The Merry Harriers* at which my *Daily Mail* cricket team regularly assembles prior to, and after, our annual match against the villagers of Hambledon, which sought to attract potential customers with a sign a couple of miles away advertising 'The Merry Harriers – Warm Beer and Lousy Food.' Bravo! The beer was precisely as warm as it ought to be and the food, if not exactly lousy, aspired to no greater pretension than the common sandwich – and the locals loved it. By way of footnote, a recent visit revealed a not inconsiderable menu of meals and more complex sandwiches and the consequent disappearance of that admirable warning down the road. Never mind, it's still a great pub – but a renewed indication that times they are a-changing.)

First, wine bar imports like quiche and stuffed potatoes began to creep into the advertised fare, closely followed by such foreign invaders as *brioches*, *panini* and *ciabatta* and finally, perhaps inevitably, the 'gastro pub'. (Panini? Ciabatta? The wife of a dear cousin of mine, upon being invited with her husband for a simple meal of 'spaghetti or lasagne or something like that,' replied apologetically: 'I'm afraid Chris doesn't eat anything that ends with a vowel.' I can almost hear the chorus of 'hear, hear' emanating from the old guard in the tap room.)

Far more closely related to the continental bar or restaurant than to the British pub, this dubious newcomer soon began to view with various degrees of hostility those customers who showed no interest in the menu, gradually relocating them into smaller and more remote naughty corners, while simultaneously denying them space on the walls to publish darts, football and cricket results, fixture lists, forthcoming pub quizzes or postcards from Ibiza.

Worse still, whenever there were insufficient lunchtime restaurant punters to justify staff wages, the absentee gastro-pub owners closed the place completely. The unthinkable had arrived – a 'pub' that thought so little of its locals that it refused to open before the early evening throughout the working week. A resident licensee, who did not pay himself or herself by the hour, would always be on duty to look after the lunchtime faithful. A paid employee, apparently, was a luxury that could not be afforded.

Next on to the diminishing stage strode Rupert Murdoch and Sky Television. Up till then, if there was anything compelling on telly, anything really demanding like *Coronation Street* or Arsenal v. Manchester United, the pub would remain largely empty until the plot was played out, whereupon thirst and an uncontrollable urge to discuss whatever had just been seen brought everyone through the door in a renewed rush of enthusiasm.

The loss by BBC and ITV of most major sporting events to Sky, still unaffordable to most households, persuaded many licensees all over the land to pay Sky large sums of money for the right to give its programmes public airing for the benefit of the disenfranchised, with the outcome that many pubs turned themselves into television stadia for the watching of soccer, cricket and rugby.

And so widespread was the arrival of TV into taverns all over the land that audiences even began assembling to watch *en masse* events that were available to them at home on terrestrial channels – thus filling large chunks of day and night with all-pervasive sporting activity, complete with demented commentary, and alienating all those for whom the local was meant to be a place for conversation and an *escape* from the tyranny of the small screen.

If that wasn't enough to split the eardrums, distract the mind of the thoughtful and bring conversation to an end within the bowels of the very institution that could arguably claim to have invented it, many publicans scored an own-goal by filling whatever brief moments of tranquillity that accidentally survived with an epidemic of interference hitherto confined to the stress-filled environment of doctors surgeries, about-to-take-off aircraft and would-be *Titanics* – canned music.

Heaven knows what was the rationale behind this ultimate assault on the senses but it was more than sufficient to spawn a magnificent reference book conceived by two worthies, Derek and Josephine Dempster, called *The Quiet Pint* and sub-titled *The Only Guide to Pubs without Piped Music*. (In an introduction to a recent edition, Julian Lloyd Webber, a man who knows better than most how to produce music and where it should be played, previews 'an even greater selection of these wonderful establishments which have bucked the trend of inflicting that most pernicious of aural pollutants – muzak – on their long-suffering customers.')

It used to take centuries to change the daily lifestyle of a nation. Mules gave way to horses. Parchment succumbed to paper. The pigeon graciously bowed to the telephone. But, by and large, progress waited until folk were ready for it. But nowadays, in the foothills of the twenty-first century, if Westminster fails to dictate serious change at least once a week it is commonly assumed that it has dozed off. Knee-jerk response has become the norm. And so, hard on the heels of this recent and frenetic epidemic of disapproval of drink, neighbourliness and conviviality, came marching the puritan hordes of the anti-smoking fraternity, waving their banners aloft.

Smokers were kicked out of pubs and forced to seek asylum on wet or chilly pavements.

All over the land, the case was put by publicans who had no aspirations to become restaurateurs that a spot of smoking amid consenting adults would not exactly bring down the walls of Jericho. No, no, responded the Parliamentarians – every city, town, village and hamlet in Britain is stacked high with decent denizens who would love nothing better than to enjoy a peaceful hour or two in the pub were it not for the cigarette smoke that polluted clothes and left eyes a-streaming.

So, with the smoking ban in place, all over Britain the hitherto discouraged non-smokers gratefully poured back to their local boozer, thrilled to be readmitted to the throbbing heart of their community?

Dream on.

All those disenchanted lobbyists who claimed they were excluded from pubs because of the dreaded weed have long since been exposed for what they truly are – non-pub people.

And the irony was that all pub regulars knew that to be the case long before the legislation came into being. Why? Because pub folk are never, by the very definition of their existence, disapprovers. If they didn't choose to share essential space with fellow creatures with whom they quite possibly disagreed on the grounds of politics, football club allegiance, nationality, sexual orientation, religion, vocabulary or even personal hygiene, they wouldn't be pub people in the first place. The last thing that would have offended them was the presence of someone puffing on something that they themselves had no need for.

The undeniable truth is that there is nobody inside who would wish them to be outside. The only ones who make that demand are not inside or outside. They are in the House of Commons. Or at home watching telly.

The next newspaper headlines to send the MPs reaching for their nut-cracking sledge-hammers were all those tales of binge drinkers falling into gutters and vomiting upon the godly.

There were two reasons, of course, why these morons – mostly highly-paid fast-trackers who should have known better and who were, more often than not, young women executives in sensible City skirts – had never been anywhere near a pub, or, at least, had left it long before they finally overdosed into absurdity.

For one thing, even towering salaries would be insufficient to get regularly and hopelessly drunk on pub prices, when the same drink was obtainable from off-licenses and supermarkets at a fraction of the price. And for another, persistent drunks are so boring and intrusive that they inevitably get kicked out, and usually barred for life, from even the roughest of boozers.

But the very existence of the bingers and their anti-social behaviour was more than sufficient excuse for successive chancellors to bang up the tax on alcohol year after year, thus sending even more punters into the supermarkets and pricing them out of the pubs, whose landlords could not afford to compete.

The people who most often had to face the reality of alcohol poisoning and its often fatal outcome knew better, of course. William Armstrong, a Norfolk coroner, confronted with yet another sad case of a drinker's premature demise, was moved to speak his mind.

'From my perspective, there's an increase in the number of deaths from acute alcohol poisoning where people have consumed massive amounts in one session and died from alcohol poisoning,' he said.

'Pubs, for the most part, encourage sensible, social drinking. Most people who have drunk themselves to death have not been drinking in pubs; they've purchased cheap drinks from super-markets. People have died from alcohol poisoning which has resulted from them spending less than £10.'

In most pubs in Britain, £10 might just about buy a single round of drinks for three or four friends. William Armstrong made those remarks as recently as April, 2011. Unfortunately, he is a coroner who knows about such things – not an MP who probably doesn't.

And over and above all its other trials and tribulations, is the British pub also fighting an enemy within?

Outside the rain fell in stair-rods. The occasional windswept pedestrian scurried past the opaque glass windows of the saloon bar under dripping umbrella. But inside the warmth of the *Myddleton Arms*, in Islington, north London, landlady Dee Canning looked after the needs of half a dozen dry and voluble lunchtime regulars.

The 'Myd' is a real pub of the old order. The pictures around the wall declare its allegiance to its Arsenal footballing neighbours – although Chelsea and Tottenham regulars enjoy the friendly badinage – and thank-you letters on the wall recognise its customers' generous support for the local St Joseph's Hospice. And Dee, who has been behind the beer pumps these past 17 years, will gladly knock up a cheese or ham sandwich for anyone needing more sustenance than the crisps, cheese biscuits, nuts or pork scratching on display.

When she took over it belonged to the Yorkshire brewing firm of Samuel Smith but it has since become one of more than 7,000 pubs in the stable of the giant Enterprise Inns. If she were allowed to, she could buy an 11-gallon barrel keg of Grolsch lager from a local wholesaler for £99.99 but is obliged to buy it from Enterprise for £130.32.The Fosters she buys for £110.78 she could pick up for £79.19 and a case of 24 bottles of Carlsberg for which she pays £13.80 would be nearly £3 less down the road. She could find even better prices at the cash and carry.

'In some ways, I'm lucky,' says Dee. 'Unlike many other pubs my contract allows me to buy a guest draught beer from elsewhere, and I buy my wines and spirits from where I want. But I pay £29,000 a year in rent and only survive because a lot of the time I look after the bar by myself.'

Certainly there are those who believe that the latest villains are not so much the legislators and the Health and Safety fusiliers but the mighty property companies that have swallowed up the nation's pubs and are holding them to ransom. And a very strong case they have.

Ironically it was yet another piece of myopic Westminster legislation that decreed that no single brewery could own more than 2,000 pubs – with the result that a massive enforced unloading means that some 18,000 now belong to the big three among the non-brewers: Enterprise Inns, Punch Pub Company and Admiral Taverns.

And whereas the brewers had a vested interest in keeping their beer outlets open for business, the 'pub-cos' shed few tears if their initial investment in a struggling local hostelry is handsomely rewarded with its sell-off as a highly expensive block of apartments.

GMB, the mighty trade union that grew out of the General and Municipal Workers and a succession of later amalgamations, has gone on the warpath, claiming that spiralling rents coupled with the price of tied beer supplies are driving many publicans out of business. And the hugely influential Campaign for Real Ale agrees.

'After first rejecting and then agreeing to investigate our complaints, the Office of Fair Trading has now decided not to get further involved,' Iain Loe, research and information manager of the Campaign for Real Ale, tells me. 'Yet there is no doubt that the individual consumer suffers from this arrangement because pub prices increase, the choice of beer is reduced, and pubs have less money available to refurbish and renovate.

'The big companies do not themselves produce beer so their only income is derived from rents, and their ability to buy cheaply from the breweries and pass on a big mark-up to the publicans. The knock-on effect is plain to see. Back in 1975, 90% of beer produced in the UK was drunk in pubs. By 1990 this figure had dropped to 79.6% and by 2008 it was 53.6%.'

Among the evidence gathered by the GMB union's 'Pub Revolution' campaign is the case of Paul Salvatori, licensee of *The Aviator*, in St Ives, Cambridgeshire. 'To stay alive you have to promote business with special events and my wife and I held a live music evening a little while back,' says the enthusiastic Mr Salvatori.

'We brought in an extra £700 in takings but by the time we had paid the band and other overheads and paid Enterprise £312 for the beer, we were left with £3.95 for our night's work. If I could have gone to the free trade for the beer it would have cost me about £190.

'Out of a turnover of £200,000, I have computed that our profit last year, excluding rent and the cost of beer, was £80,000, out of which we paid Enterprise £75,000. How long can we keep going, on just £5,000 a year spending money?'

Then came another ill-thought-out inspiration from Westminster. Let's do away with the archaic Brewster Sessions and the granting of full and occasional licenses by the local magistrates and hand the whole business over to the local council.

And what did that mindless piece of inspirational intervention achieve? Chris Churchill owns the *Half Moon Inn*, in Mudford, just outside Yeovil – as friendly and atmospheric a pub, with its beams, stone-flagged floors and scrubbed wooden tables, as you would ever care to encounter. And its range of local beers and a menu offering such comfort food as smoked haddock with cheese and chive mash, cauliflower cheese, steak and ale pie and 'exotic sausages served with mash and gravy' followed by a nice banoffee cream pie, chocolate fudge cake or warmed treacle tart, means that it is nightly packed with villagers and travellers from further afield.

Because of its success and the fact that under the new legislation its licence is now linked to its rateable value, that all-important licence which when he arrived in 2002 cost £24 for three years now costs £500 *per annum*. Having to work harder and expand to meet such overheads, the rise in his turnover means that in eight years the pub's rateable value has leapt from £6,000 to £59,900 and so his weekly council tax has now topped £1,000. And, irony of ironies, because his turnover has had to increase, he has even lost the discount he used to enjoy for being the only pub in the village.

'If you want to know why so many pubs are closing every week you need look no further than that,' says a surprisingly cheerful Chris.

And Iain Loe's colleague at CAMRA, John Howard, agreed that among all the other factors, the burden of taxation in all its forms was a key ingredient of the difficulties facing the pub trade in the 21st century.

'With the overheads getting greater and the supermarkets vying with each other to sell cheaper and cheaper, a massive disparity in pricing is creating a take-home culture throughout Britain,' he says.

'It's becoming more and more important for pubs to strengthen their role in the community, perhaps having a visiting hairdresser or becoming associated with the local football team – anything like that.

'I know of one major brewery, for example, which has even appointed a community relations manager to advise its tenants on how best to achieve this relationship.'

It turned out to be Arkells, that ages-old family brewery in Swindon, Wiltshire, and tied trade director George Arkell told me exactly why they had done it.

'We believe that about 20 per cent of our pubs are in rural places where they are the only local business still surviving after the closure of the corner shop and the post office,' he said. 'We suddenly realised that many of these landlords were so busy doing their job that they didn't have enough time left over to find out from the locals whether they were delivering what the villagers really wanted.'

The man chosen for the mission was Richard Turner, an avuncular former Arkell's director with a lifetime spent in the merchant navy and the brewing industry, who set about his job with self-confessed temerity.

'My brief was to look at 21 of our pubs which were the last remaining businesses in their village and I worried how they would react to an outsider coming in to tell them how to run their enterprise,' said Richard. 'But happily it turned out that most of them were simply delighted to discover that someone in the company was rooting for them.

'Pretty soon I discovered that of those 21, three or four were going down the drain for one reason or another, another seven or eight were not doing well and the rest were fine or only needed a little help.'

Take the *Village Inn* in Liddington, as an example. It had always been a popular spot but when Richard started talking to the locals *outside* the pub he soon discovered resentment that many of the tables in the bar were reserved for diners and the folk coming in for a drink with their mates were being crowded out. 'After a word with the landlord, tables around the bar were reallocated to drinkers only and I went back to the locals and told them that if they valued the presence of a pub in the village they really ought to support it. Since then everything has been going really well. It's often as simple as that.'

A few miles up the road, I found landlord Mark Turner's dad, Chris, in charge of the imposing *Highwayman*, a splendid, traditionally furnished watering hole in the village of Elkestone, Gloucestershire, serving good, simple food, alongside the A417 that has recently been converted from single carriageway to a dual carriageway trunk road.

'When the new road was built we asked for a slip road to allow customers to drive straight into our car park, as they could before, but this was refused so to get to us now you have to turn off on to a minor road, turn left and left again to come in at the rear,' says Chris. 'We put up signs, situated off the road in a local farmer's land, advising passing motorists where to turn off and a chap from the Highways Agency came into the pub, shouted his mouth off in front of all the customers and told us to take them down because they were a distraction to motorists' concentration.

'The signs are still there pending an appeal but if they have to go, when drivers see us by the side of the road they will actually have gone fifty yards beyond the only way of getting to us, with no way of turning back.'

'And when they recently carried out road works they closed one complete carriageway every night at 8pm for a month, despite our plea for a contraflow system.

'So people who could get to us couldn't then get home and people who could get home couldn't get to us in the first place.'

Honest to God, you have to believe it!

When we talked about the whole comedy of errors, Richard Turner said he was still trying to work out whether it was the

Cotswold District Council, the Road Management Service or the Highways Agency that had the final say in the whole absurdity.

'But there is no doubt in my mind that government, in its various forms, is responsible for killing off pubs all over the country,' he said wearily.

If I had been living and drinking in Islington, north London, rather more than 60 years ago one of my fellow 'regulars' might well have been that most eminent of pub-lovers, George Orwell.

And George – or rather Eric (Blair) as we insiders would have known him – was wont to wax lyrical about his favourite London pub, the *Moon Under Water*.

So what special ingredients recommended the *Moon* to that peerless literary prophet who was already looking towards 1984 as the year Big Brother would come to haunt us all?

Well, for one thing, its architecture and fittings were uncompromisingly Victorian – with 'no glass-topped tables or other modern miseries' and 'no sham roof beams, inglenooks or plastic panels masquerading as oak.'

The grained woodwork, the ornamental mirrors behind the bar, the cast-iron fireplaces, the florid ceiling stained dark yellow by tobacco smoke, the stuffed bull's head over the mantelpiece – everything reminded Orwell of 'the solid, comfortable ugliness of the 19th century.'

But what brought him the greatest gladness was that the house possessed neither radio nor piano, that the barmaids called everyone 'dear' rather than 'ducky', that unlike most pubs, the *Moon Under Water* sold tobacco as well as cigarettes, aspirins and stamps, was obliging about letting customers use the telephone and was particular about its drinking vessels – 'never, for example, making the mistake of serving a pint of beer in a handleless glass.'

(And I wouldn't mind betting, Eric, that the landlord would have been all too happy to cash cheques for the regulars whenever they found themselves short of the readies.)

It would not be George Orwell, however, if there was not a sting in the tail of his lyricism – the *Moon Under Water* never existed, except in his imagination… Even in his day, apparently, the rot was beginning to set in.

'If anyone knows of a pub that has draught stout, open fires, cheap meals, a garden, motherly barmaids and no radio,' he lamented all those years ago, 'I should be glad to hear of it – even though its name were something as prosaic as the *Red Lion* or *Railway Arms.'*

How cruel, to play with our senses thus! But we will not despair. Pubs have been with us for two thousand years and are surely destined to remain part of the Anglo Saxon landscape.

Oh, c'mon, surely they must be…

Chapter four

Early doors

Derby was an OK sort of place to work, full of Rolls-Royce boffins and blokes – nearly always blokes – who were building things like carriages for the youthful British Railways.

But by and large, Derby was no good for girls. For girls you had to go to Nottingham. It was only a few miles away to the east but the big difference was that Nottingham was a university city and Derby was no such thing. And universities produced girls with brains – a very challenging combination for embryo journalists with intellectual ideas above their station.

There were two approved picking up points – a couple of landmark pubs called *The Black Boy* and *Ye Olde Trip to Jerusalem*. *The Black Boy* – can you imagine a boozer with such a name in politically correct 21st-century Britain? – had few irresistible architectural qualities but it was a swinging scene and in front of it was a statue of a guy called Samuel Brunts who apparently died way back in 1711 and bequeathed this chunk of land to be used for the benefit of 'poor local people who had been industrious and of sober life and conversation and feared the Lord'. Well, at least we were poor.

Alas, the dear old *Black Boy*, with its massive central tower with dark wooden gables and a Bavarian balcony of monumental awfulness, is no longer with us – it was, apparently, knocked down to make room for a Littlewoods store sometime late in the 1960s.

But the *Trip to Jerusalem* survives and is still something else. In fact, it is a lot of things else. Apart from being a gathering place for lovely brainboxes hopefully seeking a night-time diversion from differential calculus or the dusty musings of Pliny, it has a date of

1189 on the wall outside and boasts of being the 'oldest inn in England'.

What better place, therefore, to begin a journey of enlightenment into the glorious history of the British pub? Is this really the oldest surviving home of that often anonymous army of journalists' friends lovingly known as 'sources closest to...' and 'neighbours yesterday spoke of...?'

And if so, what and where are the roadside watering holes which today fly the flag for a British institution that has somehow survived the ups and downs of more than eight further centuries?

I am about to embark on a one-man mission of discovery around the highest pubs, the haunted pubs, the smugglers pubs, the waterside pubs, the pubs that have hosted historic moments, the pubs that don't exist outside the fantasy world of television and radio soaps and a load of other pubs that just happen to be dotted around the national landscape to satisfy the common thirst.

Before entering its portals I went to have a chat with the ever-helpful Judith Edgar, keeper of community history at the Museum of Nottingham Life, which just happens to be in Brewhouse Square, right next to the *Trip to Jerusalem*.

Just what, I wondered, were the authenticated origins of the museum's distinguished neighbour? Judith, bless her, laid out a magnificent array of reference books and photo copies of ancient parchments and manuscripts on the desk between us and admitted that she had been doing her homework since breakfast.

'There are big gaps in what we know,' she began, with admirable historian's caution. 'We do know that Nottingham Castle was rebuilt in 1068 by William Peverill for William the Conqueror and that the River Lean was diverted to provide a water supply and it would certainly have been reasonable to assume that the castle would have had its own brewhouse because in those days beer was regarded as the best way of making water safe to drink. Even children used to drink a weakened form of it, known as small beer.

'What we do have is a reference to 'plague watchings' taking place 'at the brewhouse under the castle' in 1609 to 1610 and it is reasonable to assume that, if it was here then, then that is where it would have been situated when the castle was first built five centuries earlier.

'Usually a brewhouse would not only produce beer but it would also be somewhere where people could gather and drink it, but as this one was primarily for the benefit of the occupants of the castle whether they would have been encouraged to go outside the walls is open to question – I would have thought it more likely that the beer would have been delivered into the castle for consumption.'

And just how Jerusalem got into the act is equally clouded in mystery. In the language of 12th century Britain, a trip was not so much a journey as a stopping-off place during a journey, which accounts for the popular belief that the *Trip to Jerusalem* was a night's stopover for the men already recruited by Richard the Lionheart for his various crusades of the period.

But the first reference to a pub on the site that Judith can dig out was in 1760 when it was leased to a William Marriott under the name of *The Pilgrim* – a name which nonetheless suggested similar Christian outreaching – and it was not until *The Pilgrim* was sold in 1785 by auction that it was referred to in the *Nottingham Guardian* on September 3rd as the 'Jerusalem Alehouse in Brewhouse Square'.

But just to thicken the plot, contemporary references to its 'nickname of the *Trip to Jerusalem*' refer to it as being a meeting place for an obscure sect called the Philadelphians or Family of Love and of a defunct 'Court of St John of Jerusalem'.

So maybe Jerusalem doesn't refer to the crusades at all but to this mysterious court of St John of Jerusalem. All of which greatly amuses the current landlady of *Ye Olde Trip to Jerusalem*, whose name just happens to be Rosie St John…

'All I know is that I've been in this business for 20 years and if it had been the *Dog and Duck* I was looking after it wouldn't have meant anything but nowadays when I go anywhere in the world someone has always heard of the *Trip to Jerusalem*. And when visitors come here they've always done their homework and the first things they want to see are the Cursed Galleon and the Fertility Chair.'

OK, Rosie, be my guide. The cursed galleon, up in a little old bar on the top floor, turned out to be an awful, dirt-encrusted old warship in a glass bottle, crying out for the attentions of dustpan and brush. 'We don't know much about it,' said Rosie, 'but it was left here by a sailor and attached to the ceiling, which was apparently just as dirty as the ship itself – and the first three people who attempted to clean it all died gruesome deaths. So when it was finally moved, three priests of various religions were on hand to keep evil spirits at bay but the person who actually moved it had a car accident and died. From now on, it stays where it is.'

Nearby in the same room stands a pretty ordinary-looking leather chair but the notice above it explains the fascination with which it grips its visitors: 'Here sits the pregnancy chair. Legend has it that any female who dared to sit upon this ancient chair very quickly became pregnant.'

'We do get regular emails from women who tell us it worked,' says Rosie. 'But I really wouldn't know. What I do know is that our local MP, Graham Allen, sat on it about three weeks ago during Pregnancy Awareness Week and I've not heard of any remarkable outcome.'

But then, that's the thing about pubs. If they can't produce decidedly fishy stories and gloriously unprovable legends, what is the point of having them at all? In the 17th century, when stage coach travel in Britain began to grow in volume and inns sprang up solely to provide refreshment, overnight accommodation and change of horses, in the midlands town of Stony Stratford, the London-bound coach changed horses at *The Bull* and the Birmingham coach at *The Cock Inn* across the road. While this procedure was going on, passengers travelling in their different directions would exchange news, the accuracy of which was frequently found to be suspect. So suspect, indeed, that such travellers' tales became known throughout the land as 'Cock and Bull stories'.

It has been forever thus.

Anyway, not everything in *Ye Olde Trip to Jerusalem* is of fanciful provenance. The cellars, through which Rosie proudly took me on a conducted tour, really were once a cock-fighting pit, really are a hundred feet beneath the castle, really were regularly used as a condemned man's cell, and the old stone seat in the wall really was where the jailor sat and supervised his charges' last walk to be hanged outside Shire Hall.

And even if it did take me a good ten minutes to prove that it is technically impossible to succeed in the ancient game of Ringing the Bull by taking the ring at the end of a line attached to the bar wall and releasing it in such a way as to get it to come to rest around the 'horns' fixed to a neighbouring wall, it really is true that Stuart Thompson, barman at the *Trip* these past 13 years, can ring those wretched horns first time every time *while standing with his back to the target*.

But even if that 1189 date on the wall is authentic it still comes pretty late in the piece. The story of the British pub began at least a thousand years earlier than that.

> *Before the Roman came to Rye or out to Severn strode,*
> *The rolling English drunkard made the rolling English road.*
> *A reeling road, a rolling road, that rambles round the shire,*
> *And after him the parson ran, the sexton and the squire;*
> *A merry road, a mazy road, and such as we did tread*
> *The night we went to Birmingham by way of Beachy Head.*

The roads and lanes of BC Britain might well have zigzagged wildly across the land in eccentric search of the next village but the wonderful G K Chesterton would have been the first to concede that this preferred route was probably due less to the alcoholic level of their builders than to the fact that they hated hills and swamps and preferred to follow kinder contours.

If there were drunkards among them, however, their thirst was certainly slaked by the hundreds of *ale-huts* they erected along the way. Ale – beer brewed without hops – was already a British way of life and such watering holes were invariably presided over by brutish old harridans known, perhaps ironically, by the gentle-sounding name of *beldams*.

We'd been at the booze for a few thousand years already, truth to tell. Ever since the Beaker People, immigrants from north western Europe, had imported the necessary receptacles, Neolithic Brits had been filling them with a pretty potent blend of honey, water and yeast which came to be known as mead.

Cider, after a fashion, came next but it was not until the farmers learnt to cultivate grain that ale first appeared on the scene – and immediately dominated the drinking diet of perfidious Albion.

When the Roman invaders set about putting the British traveller on the straight and narrow in one respect, they certainly counter-balanced the effect in another by importing their beloved *tabernae* from back home and erecting them at generously frequent intervals along the route.

The *taberna* was, in reality, a shop that also sold wine. But Boadicea's brood recognised a good idea when it saw one and, already favouring ale to wine, recreated it as an *alehouse* and corrupted the unfamiliar Latin to *tavern*.

(The pub has always been deliciously associated with this kind of verbal evolution, of course. Way back in Berkshire schooldays, I remember becoming fascinated by the number of pubs encountered on bike rides called *The Goat and Compasses*. After some original research, imagine my delight on discovering that originally they had all been popular Puritan meeting houses called *God Encompasses Us* – obviously a bit too much of a mouthful as closing time approached. And years later, living and working in London, it was with similar pleasure that I learnt how that unlikely combo, the *Elephant and Castle* had started life more logically, if less memorably, as the *Infanta de Castille.'*)

The new arrivals, of course, intended their *tabernae* to be for the exclusive refreshment of the long-distance traveller but the natives quickly adopted their *taverns* as a bolt hole for nearby residents in search of a night out.

The local pub was up and running – and all set to play a key role in the next two thousand years of social history.

Although none of these early taverns survives in today's Britain, some of their drinking vessels later unearthed in London have been dated to around AD300 and were of pint or quart size, further indicating a trade in ale or cider rather than wine.

Sweeter and stronger than modern-day beer, the ale of post-Roman Britain was often made privately for home consumption and the early watering holes were frequently nothing more than the front rooms of houses whose owners were better at making it than others.

Some time around 970, the Anglo-Saxon King Edgar decided that the proliferation of such establishments was such that they should be limited to one per village, suggesting that these home brewers were getting much more skilled in their craft.

And it was during the same reign that over-enthusiastic alehouse indulgence was countered by a system of graded measures on the inside of wooden drinking vessels, with each quota marked with a movable peg. The accepted practice of the time was for a single mug of ale to satisfy the collective thirst of the denizens gathered in the bar and the idea, apparently, was to maintain a passable degree of sobriety by defining how much any one drinker could consume before the vessel was passed on around the table.

In the event of frequent drunkenness or other misbehaviour, the offending customer would have his permitted quantity reduced and the markers would be rearranged accordingly. He would be 'taken down a peg or two'. At least, that's the story... The pub was already at the cutting edge of English phrase and idiom.

And if *Ye Olde Trip to Jerusalem* really did open its doors for the first time as a bolt hole on the long journey to the crusades, it would at that time have been only one of hundreds of such establishments spread out across the British landscape.

How appropriate, therefore, that Chesterton's meandering tale of the Englishman and his rolling road should eventually lead to the *decent inn of death.*

> *My friends, we will not go again or ape an ancient rage,*
> *Or stretch the folly of our youth to be the shame of age,*
> *But walk with clearer eyes and ears this path that wandereth,*
> *And see undrugged in evening light the decent inn of death;*
> *For there is good news yet to hear and fine things to be seen,*
> *Before we go to Paradise by way of Kensal Green.*

Between rounds...

Once in a blue moon, if you just happen to be in the right place at the right time and the moon is blue, something happens to thrust your hitherto humble home surroundings into the world's headlines. If such an event simultaneously determines your future career and establishes a lifetime's love affair with pubs, it is additionally memorable.

DAVENPORT ARMS

Right from the time that he came back from North Africa and Italy at the end of the Second World War, and long before I was allowed to venture into such establishments on my own, my father was accepted as one of the 'back room boys' of the *Davenport Arms*, his Cheshire village local, known to everybody by no other name than The Thieves' Neck – probably because of the noose round the neck of the luckless bloke on the sign that hung over the front door.

(It is strange how often pubs are saddled with this kind of dual personality. Another place of essential refreshment near the off-Fleet Street headquarters of the *Daily Mail* was the *White Swan*, inevitably known to customers and taxi drivers alike as the *Mucky Duck*, or even just the Mucky, until it was closed for a few months to be tarted up by its misguided brewery owners, reopened and promptly rechristened the Plastic Duck, whereupon it soon disappeared altogether, and the nearby watering hole for our friends at the *Daily Mirror* was known to so many of its regulars as the *Stab in the Back* that few can today correctly identify it as the *White Hart*.)

Anyway, this particular pub was located right opposite the church in the fairly posh village of Woodford, deep in rural Cheshire but only a dozen miles south of Manchester. And its inner tabernacle – its holy of holies – was the 'Back Room'. No lady ever strayed into the Back Room because it was strictly a men-only asylum and no chap was welcomed into it, come to that, except at the specific invitation of Jack Hallworth, the landlord.

My father was honoured to be a member of this elite band of brethren and so was the much-loved, hugely respected, silver-haired vicar from across the road, the Rev Philip St John Wilson Ross.

The scene now shifts to the Llyn Peninsula in North Wales, where the good reverend and his wife, Eileen, regularly parked their familiar green trailer caravan overlooking the four-mile-long beach of Porth Neigwl – or, in rather more sinister translation, Hell's Mouth.

On the morning of Thursday, August 12, 1955, well into a glorious summer, the good vicar went for his usual early morning swim on Hell's Mouth beach and when he failed to return for breakfast his wife went out to look for him.

The rest, as they say, is history. And my word, what history!

Eileen walked first along the cliff and then down on to the beach and there discovered a neat pile of her husband's clothes. In panic, she ran to nearby Treheli, where farmer Isaac Williams was getting his cows ready for milking.

The farmer, in turn, abandoned his cows to raise the alarm and Inspector Cledwyn Shaw from nearby Pwllheli launched a massive police search, which involved coastguards, local residents, holidaymakers and even a troop of boy scouts who happened to be staying nearby.

But after three days, a distraught Eileen Ross returned to Woodford alone to grieve for her husband – finally and reluctantly convinced that he had tragically succumbed to the notorious current that gave Hell's Mouth its melodramatic name.

For more than a year the village flock slowly settled into a daily parish existence without its charismatic shepherd and the back room boys of the *Thieves' Neck* learnt to live without his cherished clerical patronage.

It was in October, 1956, that a local resident dropped a king-size spanner into the works. She somehow let it slip that she had received a letter posted in Montreux, Switzerland, from her mother, a wealthy widow by name Kathleen Ryall, in which she admitted that she was now living with the far-less-than-dead Rev Philip St John Wilson Ross, with whom she was deeply in love.

This was, of course, nearly twenty years before former government minister John Stonehouse was sensationally discovered living under a false name in Australia after apparently faking his own death in a similar 'drowning' incident on a business trip to Miami Beach and the fictional TV comedy series, *The Rise and Rise of Reginald Perrin*, utilised the same genre of deception and the impact of this staged 'death' and its daily further developments meant that life for both the village of Woodford and the *Davenport Arms* would never be the same again.

The world's press descended on the village. Even the internationally prestigious *Time* magazine in America devoted a whole page to the cause célèbre under the headline The Vanishing Vicar.

Photographers lurked in hedgerows, patiently awaiting the return in disgrace of the vicar or his mistress or both or a distant shot of the now even more distraught Mrs Eileen Ross. And in the *Thieves' Neck*, men in mackintoshes and trilby hats scribbled shorthand squiggles into notebooks, winkled out any titbits of local gossip they could lay their hands on and exchanged tales of amazing derring-do from all over the terrain of their own particular parish – which just happened to be the rest of the world.

Permitted to eavesdrop, with a glass of something non-alcoholic in hand, I immediately knew with absolute clarity how I was going to earn a precarious living for the rest of my days. School and A-levels became mere irritants to be somehow endured until real life could begin. Parental ambition that I should grace the cloisters of Oxford or Cambridge went clattering out of the window. It was to be the Loreburn Secretarial School in Manchester – with a daunting daily student population of two boys (myself and a lad called Brian Jones, sadly not the one destined to become a member of the Rolling Stones) and 437 girls, mostly armed with strange vanity boxes and long pointed umbrellas – for a diploma in shorthand and typing and a first job on a local weekly paper. And the sooner the better.

And the stage on which this volte face took place, the saloon bar of the *Davenport Arms* aka *The Thieves Neck* – mere newshounds were allowed, of course, nowhere near the 'back room' – meant that similar establishments all around the land were destined to become my spiritual homes.

I had begun a love affair with the British pub, which might have lacked the passion of that which apparently prevailed between the Rev Philip St John Wilson Ross and Mrs Kathleen Ryall but was destined to be at least equally enduring.

To complete the tale that gave rise to such a mind-blowing enlightenment on a personal road to Damascus, it turned out that our vicar was unusual as God's messengers go in that he went in to bat armed with an engineering degree. When a local Woodford businessman died back in 1951, he left behind a young wife with strikingly good looks, a country house in the village, a villa in Switzerland, a mews flat near Hyde Park in London and an engineering firm in Manchester with which she needed a spot of help to maintain. Philip Ross filled the bill and was only too willing to lend a hand.

An affair began that lasted for many years and allowed plenty of time for the planning of his final release from both the cloth and the domestic closet.

Although living in Switzerland, the spirited Mrs Ryall would return to Manchester every month on the eleventh day to sign the pay cheques for her employees. On the night of August 11, 1955, her fiscal duties delivered, she apparently drove to Llyn, stayed the night in or near Abersoch, under an assumed name, and early next day picked her lover up at the eastern end of Hell's Mouth – and hot-footed it towards London well before Eileen Ross set out on her pre-breakfast search.

The drama of Hell's Mouth and its sensational aftermath was one hell of a story but Jack Hallworth soon enough managed to settle his beloved *Thieves' Neck* back into its normally composed monitoring of local affairs.

Unknown to him, however, a die had been cast. The young William Marshall Greaves had just had the rest of his life diverted from academy and respectability into a spicy mixture of pubs and journalism.

Thank you, the Rev Philip St John Wilson Ross, from the bottom of both heart and glass.

Chapter five

Up a lazy river

So never mind the casualties – what of the pubs that have stood the test of time?

Their heritage is massive and mightily durable. Some cling to the top of mountains and windswept moorland, others perch by the waterside. Some offer city dwellers a break from the roar of traffic and the equally invasive roar of office or factory floor. Others pop up in the heart of the countryside when least expected. Some are haunted, some have played host to smugglers and highwaymen, some have made history and others have had history stamped upon them. Most have no other credentials than the asylum they offer to the denizens of an often troubled existence.

Thank God they are still there.

The accident-prone expedition up the Thames of George, Harris, J and Montmorency, the belligerent fox terrier, is so hilariously timeless that it is hard to believe that 120 years have elapsed since Jerome K Jerome immortalised the adventure in *Three Men in a Boat*.

It was strictly in pursuit of academic research, therefore, that I embarked on a pub crawl along that most tranquil of waterways to discover what impact more than a century has had on the various taverns that were honoured by their patronage.

After all, there aren't that many chances to record the evolution of the Great British Pub in such clearly defined detail.

I was sorry that Harris, in particular, could not have been at my side. He would have been in seventh heaven. ('I wonder now, supposing Harris... got to be Prime Minister, and died, if they would put up signs over the public-houses that he had patronized?' pondered J so memorably. 'No, there would be too many of them! It would be the houses he had never entered that would become famous. *Only house in South London that Harris never had a drink in!* The people would flock to it to see what could have been the matter with it.')

THE ROYAL STAG

And the faces of all four voyagers would have been wreathed in wry smiles when they renewed their acquaintance with the *Royal Stag* in Datchet and the *Manor Hotel* opposite because the last time around they lingered only long enough to be turned away.

Harris had been undismayed to be told that some rooms in the *Stag* already contained three men in a bed and cheerfully told the landlord they would gladly accept 'a shake-down' in the billiard room – only to be told 'Very sorry, sir. Three gentlemen sleeping on the billiard table already, and two in the coffee-room.'

Things seem to have shrunk a bit as the years have rolled by because Harris would be hard pushed to find room for a billiards table in the modern-day *Stag* – with or without anyone akip on its green baize.

But the whole party would be delighted to discover it is still very much a pub.

The low beams and 'Mind Your Head' warnings are as evident as ever, the wood-planked flooring polished by the feet of ages, the bar and tables clearly welcoming drinkers only, a brass footrest beneath the stools at the counter and a menu reassuringly filled with smoked haddock and mackerel fish cake, royal Windsor sausages and old fashioned beef casserole – with tiger prawn *pil pil* the only suspicious assailant from outer regions of the world.

And Montmorency's eyes would have lit up at the sight of Alfred, an English Staffordshire terrier, lying apparently asleep with his paws outstretched before him. A quick nip of one of those legs would surely have begun a thoroughly satisfactory piece of mayhem.

Keeping a motherly and fatherly eye on him were regulars Kay, William and Jerry. 'Actually they wouldn't have recognised the wooden floor because it only went in a few years ago,' said Jerry, shattering my architectural know-how. 'We used to have terrific slate slabs, which the three men would surely have approved of, but then they took them away which was a pity. But these planks are probably quite old because they came from another pub.

'And we used to have a Montmorency in the village. He was a Jack Russell who would take on anything. But Alfred here used to see him off, didn't you old boy?' The merest flick of Alfred's tail acknowledged the compliment. So no luck there, Monty.

Whatever the changes over the passing decades, here at least was a hostelry that had done its best to maintain its comforting feel of antiquity. Heavily framed pictures around the wall starred several fish, two or three horses, three grouse, a couple of pheasants and an inevitable stag at bay.

It is doubtful, however, whether our four heroes would even have bothered to wander across the road to the other scene of their rejection, then an inn called *The Manor House*. The 'House' bit has long since been replaced by 'Hotel', carpets and soft furnishings – comfortable I'm sure but another loss to the great age of the British pub.

Next stop – and an even more evident loss. To Marlow and an overnight stay at the *Crown*.

Gone. No trace. After 201 years of pulling pints for the locals, The Marlow *Crown* gave way for a kitchen showroom on Saturday, June 28, 2008. 'Dublin Dave' was there at the death. 'I always think it's sad to see so many pubs shutting down in England. Unfortunately in life they call it change – but change isn't always for the better.' My sentiments entirely, Dave.

A mile or two upstream, they would have been relieved to see their favourite pub sign still in place at the *St George and Dragon*, a few hundred yards outside Wargrave village. One side of the sign, painted by a 'Mr Leslie RA', shows the fight between man and beast at its height, and the other, by 'Mr Hodgson RA', depicts

the victorious George enjoying a well-earned pint.

Their mooring is still there but above it is a terrace full of modern, lightweight tubular chairs, and inside most of the antiquity has been revamped or replaced. Come to think about it, the sign itself has probably been saved only by Jerome K Jerome's endorsement of its artistic merit.

But reawakening today into the early 21st century after twelve decades of Rip Van Winkle oblivion, J and co would surely find the *Bull* at Sonning one of the most reassuring oases on the route of their old boys' reunion.

Back in the 1880s it was 'a veritable picture of an old country inn, with green, square courtyard in front where, on seats between the trees, the old men group of an evening to drink their ale and gossip over village politics; with low, quaint rooms and latticed windows, and awkward stairs and winding passages.'

OK, so the green, square courtyard has sadly given way to the car park that caters for the *Bull's* present-day clientele, but local gossip is still given free rein in the 'village bar' within and landlady Christine Mason insists: 'We've been here for 15 years and we have always said we would never turn the place into just another restaurant. The High Street used to have three pubs, now we are the only one, and the old *Malt House*, where they used to brew beer, is now a private house.'

Records show the *Bull* to have been an inn for more than 600 years and it boasts among its former visitors King John, en route to signing the Magna Carta and Queen Elizabeth I, but J and his fellow boatmen would doubtless be modestly chuffed to discover that, despite such exalted royal patronage, four of its five bedrooms are now called Jerome, George, Harris and Montmorency.

And they would be equally pleased to find the 'quaint little' *Swan Inn* at nearby Pangbourne much as they remembered it, even though it no longer contains the bedrooms it did in their day and seems to have grown a little towards the river. They would also doubtless be amused to discover that at some stage between then and now and despite its quaintness and littleness, it actually straddled the counties of Berkshire and Oxfordshire, requiring some of its patrons nightly to carry their pint pots from one room to the next in order to comply with permitted licensed hours.

At this stage, I hope I might be permitted a small diversion. There is no record of our three heroes venturing into the *John Barleycorn*, a few strides from the river at Goring – a pity, because they would have loved its welcoming cosiness – but it serves as my very own yardstick for measuring the endurance of the Thames-side boozer.

Rather more than half a century ago a school some eight miles away had the dubious responsibility of having me as one of its boarding students and once a term I and a couple of pals would sneak off by bicycle to the *John Barleycorn* for a highly illicit couple of pints of foaming under-age ale.

(During my last term, my housemaster enquired what I intended to do with the morrow's holiday. 'A bike ride,' said I. 'Jolly good for the muscles,' said he. 'But a word in your ear. One of my fellow teachers has taken to using the *John Barleycorn* as a stopping-off point on his travels. Might be safer to try somewhere else.' The blighter had known of my transgressions all along. No wonder I hated school.)

It was, therefore, an increasingly nervous approach. How would the passing years have treated this clandestine rendezvous? Would it indeed still be there? Would I be arrested for a string of age-old felonies? And, *mirabile dictu*, there it was, standing squat on a bend of the road, exactly as it always was. Once inside, the years simply fell away.

'Nothing changes much here,' said licensee Robert Hurst. 'I only took over as a retirement job but I was born just down the road and this is how I always remember the pub. We still have the same two bars that you would have remembered – we call them the Workers' Room and the Suited-'n'-Booted.'

And so to the village of Clifton Hampden and the *Barley Mow* – just about as far as Montmorency and his three companions ventured upstream.

Good news. Like the *Swan* further downstream, the *Barley Mow* has lost its bedrooms but the bar area, full of low beams and essential instructions to 'Duck or Grouse', is exactly as J and Co would have remembered it.

'It is, without exception, I should say, the quaintest, most old-world inn up the river,' was J's enthusiastic, comma-strewn memory of the voyagers' overnight stay there. 'Its low-pitched gables and thatched roof and latticed windows give it quite a story-book appearance, while inside it is even still more once-upon-a-timeyfied.'

Those same low beams occasioned special mention: 'It would not be a good place for the heroine of a modern novel to stay at. The heroine of a modern novel is always "divinely tall", and she is ever "drawing herself up to her full height". At the Barley Mow she would bump her head against the ceiling each time she did this.'

And even the inscriptions on the wall would surely be familiar to him: 'CALL FREQUENTLY, DRINK MODERATELY, PART FRIENDLY,' 'POOR AND CONTENT IS RICH ENOUGH,' and a rather obscure piece of history 'HOPS & TURKEYS, CARP & BEER CAME TO ENGLAND ALL IN ONE YEAR (1520).' Even if accurate, that would have been more than a century and a half after the date on the *Barley Mow* front gate – 1352.

'We serve a full menu of food but for as long as we are here people will be more than welcome just to come in for a drink,' said new licensee Paul Gover.

Not so bad then. With the *Bells of Ousley* (albeit now the *Bells of Ouzeley*) still going strong at Windsor as a Harvester Steak House, with plenty of outside tables for the thirsty, that makes one death (*The Marlow Crown*), one switch to out-and-out hotel (*The Manor House* at Datchet) and six pub survivors among the eight Thames watering holes that punctuated the intrepid threesome's upstream row.

If only the rest of the country could say the same.

Chapter six

Water, water, everywhere...

Many years ago, when the Trattoria Terrazza was the Italian restaurant that ruled the roost in Soho, its head waiter, Alvaro, took the brave decision to leave and set up his own place in the newly-trendy King's Road.

He called it Alvaro's, lost his head completely – and made it ex-directory... Who ever heard of a previously unknown restaurant, which insisted on customers having a reservation, that wasn't even in the phone book?

But he managed to tempt Princess Margaret to come and sample the fare and suddenly everyone who was anyone was striving to discover the phone number in order to book a table.

And when they made their discovery they told no one else. It was their secret and it lined the pockets of the lovely Italian adventurer.

I interviewed the guy for the *Daily Mail* and when, some months later, I repaid a debt to my father-in-law by taking him there as my guest, I insisted he chose from the finest items on both the menu and the wine list, finishing up with a liqueur of his choice.

In response to my request for the bill, Alvaro announced in a stage whisper that our meal was on him. 'Your piece was reprinted in just about every paper in Italy,' he said, 'and I've been turning people away ever since.'

Unfortunately, my dear wife's father never believed my protestations that I had no idea my 'treat' was going to be a freebie but the anecdote served to prove a marketing mystery that I realised I had stumbled across once before: The harder to find, the harder the punters strive to find it.

In an earlier life as a reporter on both the *Manchester Evening News* and the Manchester office of the *Daily Mail*, I enjoyed countless pints in *Jackson's Boat*, a friendly but unremarkable pub in the city's Chorlton-cum-Hardy district which enjoyed immense popularity – merely because scarcely anyone knew where it was.

The years have dulled the memory and all I recall is that you had to park your car at the end of a road that petered out, then walk a fair distance along an unlikely track, cross the River Mersey by footbridge and – hey presto – there it was on the far bank.

And nearly half a century later it is still there, thriving in the hands of landlord David Hall and still enjoying the custom of folk who can't quite get over the fact that they've managed to get there at all.

'Actually you can get a car right up to the door nowadays,' admits David, 'but only by driving into Trafford Water Park, going down a dip, taking a fork off to the right and pressing on for another 200 yards into the car park – a bit easier than in your day, when there even used to be a penny toll on the footbridge, but not much.'

 And if you've recently – or, indeed, ever – enjoyed a pint in the charming *Old Forge* pub on the water's edge in the tiny village of Inverie, on the mainland west coast of Scotland, south east of Skye, my word, you've deserved it. Unless you are one of the 150 inhabitants of the village, you have either trekked on foot 18 miles through the glorious but strength-sapping Munro Mountains or travelled nine miles from Mallaig by ferry, paddle steamer or canoe.

Yet mainland Britain's most remote pub remains open throughout the year and during the summer months sits 120 bums on seats every night for its simple but mouth-watering fish menu plus a fair number of punters sipping CAMRA-recommended real ale at the bar.

There can only be three explanations.

One: The harder to find, the greater the challenge.

Two: The charisma of a landlady in a million. 'We don't need the thrills of the city because it's the people who provide the entertainment here,' says Jackie Robertson, Aberdeen-born but wholly converted to the rugged charms and mountainous splendour of this wildest corner of West Scotland. 'As well as the regular visitors from afar, we have our local folk in the bar – rangers, fishermen, ghillies, farmers. We don't have a juke box, we have no fruit machines – only the chat of people who enjoy each other's company.'

And the vital third factor shared by both the *Old Forge* and *Jackson's Boat* – the eternal and irresistible pull of the water.

Without even straining, a paper pellet can readily be flicked into Loch Nevis from the three cottages that make up the *Old Forge* and the front doors of the other white-painted cottages that constitute the seafront of this idyllic hideaway, blessed by the imported warmth of the Gulf Stream, while the gentle tinkle of the infant River Mersey is similarly on hand to relax the regulars down at *Jackson's Boat*.

It is not only the three men and a dog who journeyed up the Thames 120 years ago who fell in love with the sound and sight of water – the stuff has proved an irresistible magnet for the thirsty ever since the birth of the Great British Pub.

For the people who work at the *Barge Inn* at Seend Cleeve, Wiltshire, the only downside to the pub being on the edge of the lovely Kennet and Avon Canal is that when you leave the job you are ritually thrown into the water.

It had already happened three times to 22-year-old barmaid Celine Venny when I met her in the bar a few years ago. 'The first time I was persuaded to do it for practice and the second was when I did leave,' she said with a shivery grin. 'Then I came back here and someone else left – and dragged me in with him!'

A cold experience? 'If I leave the job again, I will make sure it is in the middle of the summer.'

Well, she must have got her comeuppance at least one more time because she was no longer behind the bar when Sarah Haynes took over the licence back in 2007 – but old traditions die hard. 'We have a young student, Jack Broomfield, who works here during the holidays and then goes back to college and I've lost count how many times he has found himself in the water,' says Sarah. 'He can't mind too much, though, because he even went in voluntarily to raise money for Comic Relief.'

It was surely no accident of chance that the pub's recent glory years began in the late 1980's after a two-year-closure for major refit and enlargement by owners Wadworth Brewery, of nearby Devizes, coincided with the opening of the last group of locks that rejoined the newly-renovated Kennet and Avon to the national canal network.

'We get a huge number of narrow-boat people here, many of them calling in on both stages of their holidays and some returning year after year, says Sarah. 'And the tow path brings a steady stream of walkers and cyclists.'

All of which should be music to the ears of British Waterways, who embarked a few years ago on an ambitious £50-million plan to convert 60 identified properties alongside its 2,000-mile network into new canalside pubs.

Just such a location on the Grand Union Canal convinced Fullers, the London brewers, to convert a lock-keeper's house near Leighton Buzzard, Bedfordshire, into *The Grove Lock* pub, which opened its doors in August, 2002.

'Although we have industrial estates and a busy by-pass nearby, already a tenth of our business comes from the water and as canal-users get to know we are here this side of the business is increasing all the time,' said then-licensee Bob Shujah. 'But it does help also being next to the railway bridge where the Great Train Robbery took place.'

While new hostelries appear and others return to former prosperity along England's regenerated waterways, it is the old ones that still boast the best bar stool stories. There is the cow, for example, that fell into the Leeds and Liverpool canal and chose to swim through a mile-long tunnel before emerging to be revived with brandy by drinkers at the *Hole in the Wall* pub at Fouldridge, Lancashire. The local punters still enjoy looking at the pictures.

And regulars at the lovely 17th century *Boat Inn* at Stoke Bruerne, Northamptonshire, on the Grand Union are happy to balance their pint pots on the very table which, 200 years ago, was used as an operating table for at least one leg amputation after a gas explosion killed and injured many navvies working on the nearby Blisworth Tunnel.

A useless statistic for those who rejoice in such things: 1,400 of the 60,000 pubs in the UK are located besides Britain's navigable waterways – that's about one every three miles. Being a boatman in 18th century Britain was hard, thirsty work, however, and at its height, on some busy stretches of canal, there could have been ten pubs in a single mile.

And a few other thoughts to conjure with...

The *Navigation Inn* at Bugsworth Basin on the Peak Forest Canal was once owned by Pat Phoenix, *Coronation Street*'s Elsie Tanner. The pub is more than 200 years old and still retains its original character and atmosphere.

The highest pub on the canal network is the *Tunnel End Inn* on the Huddersfield Narrow Canal. At 645feet above sea level, the pub is the perfect place to quench a thirst before boatmen would have 'legged' through the dark and cold three and a quarter mile Standedge Tunnel.

The *King's Arms* on the River Ouse in York is a famous flooding pub. Water levels over the last 100 years are recorded and in preparation for the inevitable the beer cellar is upstairs.

The *Boat Inn* on the Sheffield & South Yorkshire Navigation near Doncaster is a former coaching house where Sir Walter Scott reputedly wrote *Ivanhoe*.

Hopwood House, a pub on the Worcester & Birmingham Canal, used to provide sleeping quarters for the 'leggers' who worked boats through the nearby tunnel. The leggers slept on benches that were hollowed slightly to stop them rolling off.

And the world's first 'drive thru' was probably the *Navigation Inn* on the Grand Union Canal near Milton Keynes which had a serving hatch that opened directly onto the canal to serve passing boatmen. The hatch is still there today although the leisurely pace of life on today's canals means that there are now mooring rings and a garden for passing boaters to stop and enjoy the break in their journey.

Meanwhile, back on the coast, it is probably the delightful *Pilchard Inn* in Bigbury-on-Sea, Devon, that can claim to be the remotest in England. If your timing is right, it is a mere 300 yards walk across the sands from the mainland to its location on Burgh Island, but for around eight hours of every tide it is cut off by the encroaching waves. Anyone deviously thinking of a phone call home with the message 'Sorry dear, I'm stuck in the pub, see you tomorrow morning' is thwarted, however, by the remarkable 'bus on stilts' which is ever on hand to take the punters back to their cars without getting their feet wet. Designed in 1969 by nuclear power station pioneer Robert Jackson in exchange for a case of Champagne, the unique Sea Tractor then cost a further £9,000 to build.

The sea gets almost as close to the *Royal Oak* in Langstone, Hampshire, lapping at its front wall at high tide but retreating so far back into the creek that separates Hayling Island from the mainland that the exposed acres of mud are home to a wonderful array of waders and other sea birds. (Not surprisingly, both the *Pilchard* and the *Royal Oak* have served as the headquarters of notorious smuggling gangs at various times in their history, of which more anon.)

But when it comes to awarding the victor's rosette to the lowest pub in Britain, the *Pandora Inn*, at Mylor Bridge, Cornwall, arguably wins it on a technicality – or, at least, part of its licensed territory clearly takes the biscuit. Spectacularly positioned at the water's edge of that part of the English Channel whose many fingers connect Falmouth to the county town of Truro, many of its outside chairs and tables are actually sited on a wide pontoon that sinks and rises with the tide. You don't get lower than that.

Chapter seven

Things that go bump

Until two or three years ago, the warm and welcoming *Anchor Hotel* and its low-beamed 17th-century neighbour, the *Ship Inn*, on the seafront at Porlock Weir in North Devon, were united under the same management and I well remember the evening I turned up to beg a room for the night.

'We only have Room 7 left, sir,' replied the landlord rather mysteriously. 'That's fine,' said I, 'because one room is all I need.' The formalities completed, newspapers ordered for next morning and a wake-up call arranged for 8am, I settled down to a well-earned pint in the bar and the book I needed to read.

(I was researching a magazine piece on the bits of Britain where fiction had become fact as far as legions of tourists were concerned and after arduous journeying around the land had arrived at the Exmoor homeland of Lorna Doone, where even the Ordnance Survey map clearly showed the whereabouts of Doone Valley.)

Several pints later, I tottered upstairs and was soon in the land of nod.

Which is still where I was when the door opened and a lady bearing a tray of tea came smiling towards me. Good lord, was it that time already? No glimmer of light edged the windows and I strained to read the time on my watch. And when I looked up my tea deliverer had vanished.

It had all been a dream and I returned thankfully to my slumbers.

That night, back in the bar, the landlord enquired after my night's sleep. 'Slept like a log,' I assured him. 'Glad to hear it,' he replied, with evident relief. 'I'm afraid we have a lady ghost who sometimes comes in to that room with a tray of tea.'

'But, oh my God, she did!' I exclaimed. 'I thought I was dreaming.'

'Sorry about that, sir,' said my host. 'I'm told that if you watched closely, you would have seen the door knob turn in the direction it doesn't turn in for anyone else but her. We've no idea who she is but you'll be all right tonight because she's never been known to turn up two mornings on the trot.'

Honest.

(Nowadays the gloriously antiquated, low-beamed *Ship Inn* looks like it ought to have a resident ghost but doesn't have a Room 7 – although its glamorous manager, Steph Thornton is among several who think they have encountered a non-tea-tray-carrying lady ghost hovering around the place – and the response from the lady I spoke to at what is now called *Millers at the Anchor* was instantaneous: 'If she's still here, I'm off!' So maybe she just didn't like the alterations and moved on to pastures new.)

Thirty-odd years go by and, in the course of researching this humble celebration of the British Pub, I checked in at the *Speech House* inn in the heart of the wonderful Forest of Dean, between Gloucester and the Welsh border, to investigate its pivotal role in the unfolding of English history – of which more anon.

Next morning I found myself chatting to the hostelry's new and charismatic owner, Peter Hands, and told him how I proposed to devote one instalment of my epic to the haunted pubs that maintained a spiritual link with their own individual history.

'Well, we're haunted as well, you know,' said Peter, a tad uncertainly – 'or so my wife and daughter tell me. On separate occasions recently they both stayed in the same room and first my wife heard a strange tapping which seemed to come from right alongside her bed and before she could finish her account my daughter chipped in and said that, yes, she heard exactly the same and it was in the early hours before any of the staff would have been around in the corridor.'

'So they would have been in Room 8,' said I.

'How do you know?' – 'Because I was in Room 8 last night,' I explained, manfully trying not to display the chill that had suddenly enveloped me. 'I got up to have a pee and when I got back into bed I suddenly sat up because someone was in the room with me. I could swear I heard a tap-tap on the floor or wall. But then everything went still and I thought I'd imagined it.'

'What time would that be?' – 'Five o'clock – I looked at my watch.'

'Yes, my wife and daughter both said it was about five.'

Was I, I wondered, going bonkers? 'Oh, I'm the ultimate cynic,' agreed the sympathetic Peter – 'or, at least, I *was*. But before buying this place, we used to own *The Bell* at Tewksbury. There was a penthouse room and so many people said they heard the disembodied voices in there which, from snatches of their words, seemed to belong to about twenty 'lost souls' who had come through the Wars of the Roses and for some reason were dragged out to the mill in the grounds and hung, drawn and quartered that, in the end, I asked the local vicar to come and put them to rest. After his visit no one heard them again.'

The incomparable Noel Coward sang of the stately homes of England and how, albeit 'rather in the lurch,' they nonetheless 'provide a lot of chances for psychical research.'

> *There's the ghost of a crazy younger son*
> *Who murdered, in thirteen fifty-one,*
> *An extremely rowdy nun*
> *Who resented it.*
> *And people who come to call*
> *Meet her in the hall.*
> *The baby in the guest wing,*
> *Who crouches by the grate,*
> *Was walled up in the west wing*
> *In fourteen twenty-eight.*
> *If anyone spots the Queen of Scots*
> *In a hand-embroidered shroud*
> *We're proud of the Stately Homes of England.*

Brilliant stuff but with all due and sincere respects to the Master (whom I once interviewed in Manchester and who called me 'dear boy' throughout – I loved it), if he were alive today he would certainly encounter more disembodied spirits in the historic pubs and inns of Britain than he would in the nation's stately homes.

And if he really yearned to exchange a few home truths with Mary Queen of Scots he would be better advised to pop in one evening to *The Talbot* in Oundle, Northamptonshire, than seek an invitation from any of our hereditary nobles.

As well as staking a viable claim to being on the longest continuous site of any pub or inn in Britain – *The Tabret* was opened as a hostel in 638AD and was completely rebuilt on exactly the same spot nearly a thousand years later to be renamed the *Talbot* – it is also the home of one of the most remarkable ghost stories of them all.

Ten years after it was rebuilt, the staircase from nearby Fotheringhay Castle was removed and reinstalled in the *Talbot* and to this day takes residents from near the bar to the second floor bedrooms.

What many of those residents do not know when they ascend those ancient stairs is that the mysterious outline of a crown on the polished wood of the balustrade is believed by historians to be the imprint of the ring worn by Queen Mary as she gripped it for support while being escorted down that same staircase on the way to being beheaded at the command of her cousin Queen Elizabeth I, in February, 1587. And a small wooden gate still to be found on the staircase marked the limit of her freedom while under house arrest at Fotheringhay.

…Which doubtless explains the frequent sightings of Mary standing serenely at the head of the staircase and within a neighbouring room more than 400 years later. With such reliability does she make her reappearance, apparently, that Beth Fretwell, the inn's general manager, holds 'fright nights' three times a month, to enable various groups to say how-d'you-do to her luckless majesty.

(By way of macabre coincidence, the executioner who was given the job of beheading Mary lodged at the *Talbot* the night before and 'partook of pigeon pie, drank a quart of best ale and made a merry discourse with the serving girl 'til the early hours of the morning.' Fortunately for the inn's harmonious spiritual relations he does not today choose to revisit the location of his brief but memorable stay.)

But if you are perceptive to sharing a moment or two with the disembodied, you'll be positively crowded out in the gruesomely-named *Bucket of Blood* pub in the village of Phillack, alongside the once-powerful port of Hayle on the North Cornwall coast. (A couple of hundred years ago, the then landlord went to draw water from the well but instead was confronted by a bucket of blood. A headless corpse had been thrown down the well, but who and by whom has never been discovered.)

Hearing tales of weird encounters, including the appearance of a ghostly bishop, banging doors on calm days, moving furniture and creaking floorboards, a band of switched-on enthusiasts called the Paranormal Research Organisation recently asked if they could spend the best part of the night locked away in the low-beamed pub.

Over a pint of ale, I read its report with growing wonderment. 'Our psychical team had no prior knowledge yet came up with the following presences,' it began.

And get a load of this. The 'presences', in no particular order, included a man murdered in the cellar, a previous landlord who repeatedly walked across the road, a young man in the kitchen, an old woman in the bar, a cat and dog lurking in the garage, two nine-year-old girls smelling of rabbits in the bar and a one-eyed man called Jack sitting by the bar counter.

Landlord Richard Shackleton was able immediately to pour light on the identity of the last of the visitors. 'That would have been the man with one eye who used to drink in here every night until he died,' he told the investigators. 'He used to sit on the very seat where your chap encountered him.'

Elsewhere in the land by no means all the spirits have optics sitting beneath them.

Pop in for a pint or two at the lovely old *Punchbowl Inn* in the village of Lanreath, in Cornwall, and it won't be long before you hear the story of the vicar, his wife and the amorous curate. Seems the old vicar found himself out of wine in the vicarage, popped down to the cellar, slipped and fell to his death. Slipped or pushed? The curate duly took over the parish, with the vicar's widow at his side, but when a huge black cockerel appeared to terrorise the village, the locals had no doubt that it was the reincarnation of the cuckolded minister returned to reek his revenge.

Eventually, the locals caught the cockerel but it escaped and flew through a window of the *Punchbowl*, down the stairs into the cellar kitchen and into the oven. The landlord slammed shut the door at the head of the stairs and although strange things have beset the pub ever since – such as the vacuum cleaner that regularly unplugged itself when no one but its user was in the room – the cockerel has remained imprisoned ever since.

'That door will remain locked as long as I'm here,' the current landlady told me, with a barely discernable shiver. In its long history, the pub has been coaching inn, courthouse and distribution centre for local smugglers' contraband, well used to separating the villainous lower classes from the local landlords, and its bars are today appropriately called the Men's Kitchen, the Farmers' Kitchen and 'The Snug (Ladies welcome)'. But cockerels are still strictly out of favour.

Although the current manager of *The Birdcage* in Thame, Oxfordshire, has been undisturbed these last 18 months, she has to assume that her ghostly residents are merely having an elongated nap. Because former landlady Pat Neville had no doubt that a top bedroom was still haunted by one of the town's lepers who were once incarcerated there.

After several guests announced they were too frightened by the knockings and other sounds they heard during what should have been the quiet hours of night to want to stay in the building again, and even her own family were beginning to get the collywobbles, she decided enough was enough.

'I felt a real Charlie speaking out aloud in an empty room,' she said, 'but I felt I had to do it. I said "You are beginning to frighten my children. I don't mind you being here, as long as you don't hurt anybody..." Strangely enough the knocking seemed to stop for a while after that.'

The spectacular stone vaulted bar of the *Lord Crewe Arms* in Blanchland, Northumberland, one of only five Grade I listed villages in the country, certainly looks like the kind of place where the odd ghost should lurk – and nor does it disappoint.

This was once the home of General Tom Forster, who led the ill-fated Jacobite Rebellion in 1715 without ever having the necessary qualifications for the task. After his surrender he was imprisoned and was awaiting trial for high treason when his heroic sister Dorothy rode to London in disguise, orchestrated his escape, brought him back to Blanchland and hid him in a priest hole until he was able to flee to France.

Nowadays guests are still surprised when the ghostly Dorothy confronts them from time to time with a polite request to take a message to her brother.

But just whose hand print regularly appears on the top right pane of the window facing the church in the *Royal Stag* at Datchet no one can be quite sure, although, from its size it is believed to be that of a child who died in the churchyard while waiting for his father on a cold night. What is for certain, however, is that no amount of rubbing can get rid of it before it is ready to disappear of its own volition. And here comes the really creepy bit – when the pane was removed and replaced with new glass, still the handprint repeated its occasional appearances. In 1976 someone was alert enough to get a photograph of it, which today hangs on a wall in the pub.

THE WHITE HART

But there can surely be few more persistent spiritual regulars than 'Old George,' who is such a frequent occupant of his favourite stool at the bar of the 300-years-old *Drovers Inn*, at Inverarnan, near the northern tip of Loch Lomond, that more than one guest has made special reference in the visitors' book to the friendly gentleman who entertained them with anecdotes from yesteryear – apparently unaware that they were talking to a ghost. (And even when he's not holding forth he's very much in the vicinity because he loved the pub so much that his last request was to have his ashes kept in an urn behind the bar.)

Although she didn't make an appearance after the night I stayed there, a young lady who was jilted at the altar and died heartbroken, is still regularly to be seen waiting for her wedding breakfast at the charming *Castle Inn* in Castleton, Derbyshire, and regulars sitting along the padded wall seats of the cheery, low-beamed *White Hart* in Chalfont St Peter, Buckinghamshire, are always glad to welcome nineteenth century former landlord Donald Ross whenever he chooses to pay them a return visit.

They can't actually see him, but they can hear the melodious sounds of the fiddle with which he used to entertain his regulars in days of yore.

'Well, that's not quite true,' amended licensee Rachael Bree. 'I have actually seen him once in 22 years and my cleaner once in 30 years. But we hear his hob-nailed boots pacing across the landing every day and his fiddle at least once a week. The snatches of music only last a few seconds unfortunately – not long enough to get everyone dancing around the bar.'

There's always a friendly reception at the fireside of the traditional British Pub – even if you happen to have been dead for a few hundred years.

Chapter eight

Getting high

I was on *Daily Mail* business when I checked in for a night or two with my old chum, Andrew Burrell, landlord of *The Board* in Hawes at the windswept top end of Wensleydale in the North Yorkshire Pennines.

At the time, *The Board* was the busiest of four pubs in one of the highest market villages in England – if for no other reason than the local vet was offered a free lunch every market day and Dales hill farmers flooded in behind him because they preferred free consultations to the ones you had to pay for. If you run a rural pub always make sure you look after the vet and the rest of the business will look after itself.

Any road, as we say thereabouts, I had a day off and asked Andrew where was my best starting point if I wanted to climb Ingleborough, one of Yorkshire's famed Three Peaks.

'You start at the *Hill Inn*,' said he. 'It's run by an old mate, Alan Greenbank, and if you can't find it, just ask anyone to direct you to the pub where the dog does the washing up.'

Where the dog does the washing up? Was I mishearing or was this the newspaper picture spread to end all picture spreads?

The next lunchtime I duly introduced myself to Alan and asked him whether there was any truth in what I had heard. By way of answer, Alan put eight pint beer mugs with handles into the sink behind the bar, placed a bar stool beneath the basin and turned on the taps.

As soon as the water began to flow, from behind us the kitchen door burst open and, in a streak of fur, a Jack Russell terrier shot by, leapt on to the stool, buried his head in the fast-filling sink and emerged with the first glass in his teeth, which he duly shook and placed on the draining board beside him.

Seven more times he repeated his task and, upon satisfying himself that the basin was now empty of glassware, dipped his head yet deeper to emerge with the plug in his mouth, which he wrapped round the taps and, without a backward glance, returned to his basket in the kitchen. Job done.

(The beloved dog's younger brother or sister – I can't remember which – was showing a keen interest in becoming a deputy washer-upper at the time. 'I certainly don't need two of them,' said Alan. 'I've offered a tea towel and suggested I could do with a dog to tackle the drying but so far it has fallen on barren ground.')

Did that centre spread ever appear in the *Daily Mail*? It did not. Upon my request, a photographer from Manchester spent the next three days making daily trips to this remote pub only to discover the dog was strangely off colour. And his fourth visit was to learn of the dog's untimely death.

(At about the same time, my colleague and chief football writer at the *Mail*, Jeff Powell, told me of the elephant, resident in the zoo at Monte Carlo, who never missed a moment of the action whenever Monaco had a home game. The zoo was immediately next to the football ground and the elephant would put his trunk over the dividing wall as the whistle went for the start of the first half and would remain transfixed until half time, when he would go for a quarter hour stroll but never fail to be in position for the start of the second half, which he watched intently throughout before accompanying the ref's final whistle with a far louder trumpet of his own. I rang the curator who confirmed Jeff's story. You've guessed it. Elephants live for a great many years but this one sadly passed away before I could reach the principality. Don't ever tell me an animal story – not unless you wish the poor creature a premature demise.)

The memory of what so nearly was a notable scoop was, however, more than sufficient excuse for me to return to the *Hill Inn* at the start of a tour of some of the highest and most desolate pubs in Britain, to see how they are adapting their historical purpose to 21st century survival.

Alan Greenbank had long since retired but current landlady Sabena Martin – known to all the faithful as Bean – listened patiently to my rambling tale of the washing-up dog. 'We've got two remarkable dogs here ourselves,' she said, rather dismissively. 'One of them, a 14-year-old springer-collie cross called Maurice, has been awarded the National Park's Ingleborough Medal for his amazing one-dog unaccompanied expeditions. He must have made at least 50 trips around the Ingleborough and Pen-y-Ghent mountainsides and he never comes home – but he never gets lost either. He just checks in at one of several favoured addresses where he knows we will be rung up to organise his collection.'

And the other remarkable dog? 'Oh yes, that's Peggy, our two-year-old Airedale. She sings.'

She does too. The duet she offered with her mistress was truly astonishing in its melodic range. You couldn't make it up. If you don't believe me, go have a sing with her. No wonder I love pubs.

During the summer months, Sabena and husband Colin – a former chef and pastry cook at the Ritz Club in London, whose amazing sugar sculptures, on view around the pub, number the Queen, Michael Jackson, Elton John and the Sultan of Brunei among their collectors – are inundated with walkers, climbers and tourists but need all their ingenuity to keep going through the winter.

'We have started doing special evenings like tapas nights to bring people in and we organise domino nights in conjunction with the *Station Inn* at Ribblehead, just up the road, where we collect money for local causes like the scouts and the air ambulance,' says Bean. 'We're doing our level best to keep afloat.'

Set off in the opposite direction from Hawes, traverse the dramatic Buttertubs Pass into Swaledale and start climbing towards the head of Arkengarthdale along a road that stretches like borderless grey tape stuck to the undulations of those bleak but majestic fells and after a while, silhouetted against the skyline and several miles from the nearest other building, you get your first glimpse of the *Tan Hill Inn*, at 1,732 feet above sea level the highest pub anywhere in Britain.

Your car will never be alone in the car park. At any time of day or night it will be accompanied by at least one other vehicle – a bright orange articulated snowmobile with two sets of caterpillar tracks whose presence somehow defines the awesome hostility of the surrounding landscape more eloquently than any words could achieve.

But step inside and the warmth hits you amidships – and it does not only come from a roaring fire. Owner and landlady Tracy Daly's irrepressible good humour somehow pervades every inch of the bare stone flooring, the wooden planked tables, the bar stools and the children's paintings on the ceiling to reduce the shivers to a distant memory.

And the brass plates along the edge of the bar counter, adorned with unpunctuated capital letters, are guaranteed to bring a smile to the most reluctant face.

BULLSHIT CORNER... FAULTS I MAY HAVE BUT BEING WRONG ISN'T ONE OF THEM... JESUS LOVES YOU EVERYONE ELSE THINKS YOU ARE A PRAT... NO THERE'S NO F IN PARKING... HOW TO AVOID A HANGOVER STAY DRUNK... NO BLOODY SWEARING... and my favourite: A FRIEND IN NEED IS A PAIN IN THE ARSE.

'They were all there when we arrived and we didn't even think of taking them down,' Tracy told me later.

('They were probably put there by the previous owner,' says Tracy's other half, Mike. 'At first meeting he appeared a bit on the rude side but you got to like him more and more as time went by. I'll never forget his first words when we went to look at the place. He was standing warming his arse in front of the fire and he looked me up and down and said "How does an old fart like you end up with a young bird like her?" They were 64 and 46 respectively when I met up with them – just thought you'd like to know.)

It was a chance visit to *Warren House*, a similarly remote watering hole on top of Dartmoor (of which more later) which launched Mike and Tracy – both recently second-time-arounders – on to a pub crawl around the highest boozers in the land.

'And It was in the November of 2004 that we got as far as the *Tan Hill*,' recalls Mike. 'We had both given away everything when our former marriages ended and were living in a caravan but Alex, the owner for about 12 years, had decided to sell up, was asking £500,000 and we borrowed the money to buy it. As a tunnelling engineer, I had a decent income but Tracy, who doesn't drink and doesn't like drunks, became the hands-on boss.'

They had no delusions about their new environment. In the winter of 1947 the Tan Hill Inn had been cut off from the outside world from early January to the end of March and still relies on its own water bore hole, Calor Gas and generators for all the utilities necessary for everyday survival. 'When we were snowed in over New Year recently, we, our two members of staff who happened to be on duty when the snows came, and all the resident guests – we have seven letting bedrooms – clubbed together and drew up lists of volunteers every day to look after preparing the veg, washing up and even cleaning the lavatories,' recalls Tracy.

The barn that was meant to house Mike's small collection of historic 1920s tractors became the first casualty when Tracy decided it had to become a functions room – complete with licence to stage weddings.

And the pub that had begun life as the *Beer House* to attend to the thirst of 12th century coal miners and which much later became one of the many resting places for Dick Turpin after being chased out of York along the old Jagger Road, which happened to pass the Tan Hill, and, later still, fell into the hands of the legendary Susan Peacock, who ran it from 1903 to her death in 1937 – 'She not only carried a gun but could shoot straight' – entered a new phase in its fight to keep pace with changing times.

Nowadays, delighted visitors frequently find themselves passing the time of day in the bar with any one of Mike and Tracy's five cats, four dogs, two pigs, eight hens, 5 alpacas, eleven sheep and two horses – 'the health and safety people don't like it much but you can't stop them wandering in from time to time to warm themselves by the fire' – and windscreen-ticketing operations around a radius of many miles bring in a regular supply of punters for a whole variety of special events, even including mediaeval recitals.

'It began as a hobby but pretty soon became a business,' says Tracy. 'You can't live on being the highest pub in Britain alone, even if we do have the added bonus of being a natural stopping-off place for walkers along the Pennine Way. However you do it, you have to strive to be unique in one way or another to survive in this business.'

(When Tracy advertised a Christmas 'family feast' and was astonished to receive a letter from Kentucky Fried Chicken's lawyers, demanding a change of description because 'family feast' was a KFC registered trademark, she immediately rang them to point out that her business was at least 45 miles from the nearest KFC outlet and that 'you have no right to hijack the English language anyway.'

'When they refused to back down, I invited ITV to come and cover the dispute – we even got hold of a KFC bucket to shake in front of the cameras – and after it appeared on screen we must have got three thousand emails from all over the world congratulating us on our stand. KFC did back down after that and it certainly didn't do our trade any harm. Once again we were back on the map.' Not a lass to mix with, our Tracy.)

If missing out marginally on altitude, five other pubs certainly vie with the Tan Hill Inn when it comes to high level remoteness – *The Cat and Fiddle* between Macclesfield and Buxton, the *Lion Inn* on top of the Yorkshire Moors, the *Kirkstone Pass Inn* between Ullswater and Ambleside in the Lakes, the *Warren House*, perched in utter desolation near Postbridge on Dartmoor in Devon and the highest pub in Wales, the *Sportsmen's Arms*, near Bylchau in Snowdonia. (The highest boozer in Scotland, the *Wanlockhead Inn* near Biggar, bucks the trend by being mostly brand new and sitting snugly in the middle of the country's highest village, but then that's typical of Scotland – it's got to be different.) All in their different ways use imaginative enterprise to bolster their fight for survival.

Drive north out of the picture postcard village of Hutton-le-Hole, high in the North Yorkshire Moors National Park, with its pristine white-painted fencing and gurgling stream, and travel ever northwards and upwards for several miles and if you are lucky enough not to be engulfed in low cloud you eventually see the *Lion Inn* on the distant skyline.

It's been there for some 500 years as a travellers' port in a storm and Gaynor Dent has been its manageress for the last 15 of them – running a staff quite capable of serving 800 meals on a single busy day.

'We don't have many locals, of course, but we do get coach parties from as far away as Scarborough, Leeds, Halifax and we have 13 guest bedrooms so the bar is usually pretty busy,' she says. 'We have walkers on both the Coast to Coast path and Lyke Wake walk across the North Yorks Moors, we're very dog friendly and we even have a friendly ghost. His name is Tommy, who was apparently an alcoholic from Middlesbrough who loved his dominoes. He doesn't bother anyone and I've often heard someone saying to a friend 'don't worry, it's only Tommy' before ordering up another pint.'

And the sign behind the bar again contributes an entertaining addition to the litany of pub humour: LOST DOG – 3-LEGGED – BLIND IN ONE EYE – MISSING LEFT EAR – BROKEN TAIL – RECENTLY CASTRATED – ANSWERS TO LUCKY.

Oh, all right then, but on a dark, windy night any little giggle helps to lift the spirit.

I've often passed enchanted hours in John Norris' huntin' shootin' and fishin' emporium in Penrith on my journey north to Scottish salmon rivers, but never before, as far as I remember, had I taken the road west from Penrith to Ullswater and beyond that ends up climbing into the stratosphere over the wild and rugged Kirkstone Pass. Most certainly, and inexcusably, I had never popped into the *Kirkstone Pass Inn* at the very summit. And by the time I encountered landlady Beverley Llewellyn she was looking a shadow of her former self. 'it's the first time all day we haven't had a queue five deep at the bar,' she said – 'Where have they all come from?'

It was a balmy midweek day deep into October and the crowds at the tables in the garden were mostly in short sleeves, so I invited her to answer her own question. 'Well we collect the water ourselves from the fell, there's two diesel generators, Calor Gas, a sceptic tank and we have no TV reception or signal for mobile phones so it can't be the modern amenities that drags them in,' she said with a huge grin.

So who were all these punters? 'We have three double rooms and one triple and we get people who come back year after year for those – for some reason quite a few of them come from Blackpool,' she said. 'And the rest are mostly tourists although Daryl Hardy here is our only regular.'

(Oh, and why would that be, Daryl? 'I only come to see Bev,' he admitted unblushingly. OK, so that doesn't count then. The pub has no locals.)

It was Lakeland's favourite son, William Wordsworth, who described this resting place for the weary as a 'small public house recently built' in 1846 but from then until the mid-20th century it was known to one and all as the *Travellers' Rest*. And it was only built in the first place because of the number of deaths among storm-stricken walkers at the behest of the larger-than-life foxhunting Parson Sewell of nearby Troutbeck.

Seems the good William Sewell, albeit headmaster of Keswick Grammar School on days he couldn't find anything to shoot, nonetheless found time to attend to his grebe lands in these parts and famously responded from the pulpit to a parishioner desperate for rain for his crops with the less-than-helpful counsel: 'No use praying for rain while t'wind's in this quarter' whereupon he announced the next hymn. They tend to be a bit like that hereabouts.

While learning shorthand and typing at night school, I took a daytime job at a screen printing mill in Macclesfield. Nothing too demanding – I remember taking rolls of silk, spiking them to and fro on a couple of pins sticking out of the wall a yard apart, counting the folds and writing the total yardage on the end of the cloth. I also collected the tea from the canteen twice a day.

Amazingly, amid this frenzied activity, I retained sufficient energy to take a young girl co-worker in my erratic pre-war MG car up to the *Cat and Fiddle* pub at the top of the Buxton road for a glass of something or other every lunchtime. Ah, the resilience of youth.

It's still there, indisputably the second highest pub in Britain and miles from anywhere, serving the needs of the intrepid – just like it did in the days when Charles Rolls and a few cronies used to motor up there on a regular basis in the first decade of the 20th century with his brainchild, the early Rolls-Royce roadster, dragging logs behind it along the tarmac to prove its reliability.

In the seven years he has hosted the *Cat and Fiddle*, only for four days in the winter of 2010-11 was current manager Ben Davenport forced to admit defeat and close the pub. 'One of my previous licensees actually froze to death here and another employed a staff that included Albert Wilshaw, ostler and groom, so I suppose life is a bit simpler now,' he said..

There's been a pub of sorts on top of Dartmoor for nigh on 900 years but the current *Warren House* was built as recently as 1845 for the very practical reason that the local tin miners needed somewhere to wet their whistle.

And ever since that day the fire has burned non-stop in the saloon bar – 165 years without a single firelighter. And never was it more welcome than in the winter of 1963 when snowdrifts 20 feet high cut it off from the outside world for 12 weeks, with essential supplies being flown in by helicopter.

Nowadays landlady Janet Parsons tempts what few locals there are with such delicacies as homemade pork sausages and her famous treacle tart. 'The tin miners have long gone and now our customers are walkers and car drivers,' she says. 'We keep in plenty of food and gas and just pray that the generators keep going.'

Bob Hughes and his wife Bethan have been running the *Sportsman's Arms* – at 1,600 feet, Wales's highest pub, situated under the distant shadow of Snowdon, for the past 17 years – 'it's isolated on the moor, windswept and often pretty frightening, and I don't suppose many people thought we'd last out this long,' says Bob, 'but we're both from the Denbigh Moors and we knew what we were taking on.'

Drive up the meandering A5 through the verdant foothills of Snowdonia and turn off a few miles short of Betws-y-Coed, climb into the dramatic, windswept moorlands that lead over the tops towards Denbigh and pretty soon you see the pub silhouetted in glorious isolation against the horizon.

Step inside and you know for sure that mine host is a man in his element. No idle city escapee, Bob's day job is a sheep farmer hereabouts, his two sons helping on the farm, his wife, Bethan, in charge of the kitchen and their three daughters serving on – a travellers' watering hole with a true family welcome.

And if you ask him nicely, Bob will produce a newspaper cutting which is his wife's lasting accolade: 'One must cut one's cloth outside London. Don't look for urban haute cuisine, but the Sportsman's Arms on the A453 at Bylchau boasts the best steak and kidney pie I have eaten for a long time.' The byline picture at the top of the article is that of the magnificent and unmistakable Clarissa Dickson-Wright.

The Hughes have a cottage in the grounds which houses longer-stay residents as well as overnight bed and breakfasters and local farmers bring their families for regular meals. 'But mostly we rely on visitors from further afield, with one luckless volunteer steering clear of the booze to drive home,' he says. 'And reliant on our own well, at least we don't have a water bill to pay'

At 1,531 feet above sea level, the *Wanlockhead Inn*, high above Biggar, in Scotland, is unchallenged as the highest pub in Scotland, but unlike its counterparts in England and Wales, it is surrounded by the 350-strong population of the highest village in the country and has been a pub only since early this century.

But some of the pub used to be the kitchen of the Duke of Buccleuch's hunting lodge, before his grace donated it to the local branch of the Royal British Legion. 'It was then turned into a pub after the only other pub in the village, the *Mountain Lodge*, that was actually even higher by a few feet, went out of business,' says landlord James McKelvey. And James' tavern may be a new arrival but the village is no stranger to history. Not only is the 10th Duke the richest and grandest descendant of all Charles II's illegitimate offspring but the locally mined gold – all 22.8 carats of it – features prominently in the Crown Jewels and the ceremonial mace of the Scottish parliament. 'We built the new front of the pub but the village of Wanlockhead is mighty proud of its past,' says James.

But despite being in the middle of a village and being the highest pub in Scotland, the *Wanlockhead Inn* does not have the honour of being the loftiest village pub in Britain. That distinction belongs to the quirkily-named *New Inn*, standing proud at the heart of the windswept cluster of houses that make up the village of Flash, not that far from the *Cat and Fiddle* off the Buxton to Leek road in the Derbyshire Peak District.

'I don't know how it got its name in the first place but it's far from being new – it's certainly been a pub for at least 150 years,' says landlady Diane Phillips. 'I stopped doing food a while back because the cost of a cook was more than we could afford, but we put in a pool table and we now belong to a league with about fifteen other pubs and that brings in a lot of regular business.'

With its stone-flagged floor and original joists above and the warmth of Diane's reception to each windswept new arrival, the *New Inn* looks every inch the bastion against the ferocity of nature and the centre of a resolute community that has been the role of the British pub for twenty centuries.

As a small child brought up somewhere near the top of the Pennines, I have vivid memories of digging through snow higher than my head to get to the outside loo. The highest pubs in Britain look down on such lowland irritations. They are the last of the great survivors. Long may they keep pulling the pints.

Chapter nine

Where did you get that name?

A week or so after I joined the *Stockport Advertiser* as a trainee and utterly bewildered reporter a plane carrying the entire Manchester United football team, its manager Matt Busby and a number of leading sports writers crashed on take-off at Munich airport.

Nearly all the fatalities, including the wonderfully gifted Duncan Edwards, already popularly crowned as the finest footballer in the land, lived in our parish and among those of my colleagues immediately assigned the gruesome task of knocking on the doors of the bereaved families was Ian Gregory, rather older than the rest of us because he came to his new journalistic career with an unusual qualification – a BA degree in theology at Manchester University.

So what has this to do with the great British pub? Bear with me.

As the years rolled by, my former ally rose to become editor of the *Solihull News* before rediscovering his former vocation and being ordained the Rev Ian Gregory, with a ministry in Newcastle-under-Lyme.

Much more memorably, however, he became so upset by a diminishing standard of common courtesy and the resultant damage such incivility was doing to the fabric of community life that he formed an organisation – local at first but soon receiving national status – which he christened the Polite Society.

With no less a patron-in-chief than the Duke of Devonshire, the Society launched several annual Days of Courtesy – 'Think of Someone to Thank' was one notable battle cry – and Ian became a regular interviewee on such mass media outlets as the *Today* programme on Radio 4.

After 20 years leading his flock – '667 sermons, 93 marriages and 140 funerals were about enough for any man' – he retired in 2002. But not before a disused local insurance office had been bought and turned into a pub and the new brewery owners, discovering the fame of one of its potential regulars, called it *The Polite Vicar* and invited Ian to pull the first pint.

And that's where we were when we met up again recently to chew over our absent years. 'A pint of Greene King for me, please,' I said to the attractive young lady behind the bar, 'and the polite vicar will have the same.' When the story behind this strange request was revealed, the barmaid was so overwhelmed she almost offered us the drinks on the house.

It's not often that anyone gets the chance to slake their thirst with the very man or woman who features on the pub sign outside and my chest positively heaved with pride. ('I actually held two christenings over in that corner of the bar,' revealed Ian. 'One or two Christian organisations objected but many people who are a bit frightened of going into a church feel much more at home in a pub and if we can reach them there, so much the better, don't you think?')

So that's how one Great British Pub came by its name and we've already disclosed the origins of the *Cat and Fiddle* (Caterine la Fidele, Catherine of Aragon, first wife of Henry VIII), the *Elephant & Castle* (Infanta de Castille, Edward I's missus) and the *Goat & Compasses* (God Encompasses Us) but how's about the *Drunken Duck*, in glorious countryside at Barngates, near Ambleside and not far from the banks of Lake Windermere?

I was enjoying a quick pint of Cracker Ale, brewed on the premises and named after the family Jack Russell Terrier, when owner Steph Barton told me the delightful story. Seems that way back in Victorian times the then landlady came across her ducks stretched out in the roads and, although saddened by their demise, set about plucking them in readiness for the oven. She had almost finished her task when one of them gave a pronounced wriggle of protestation.

'A barrel had apparently slipped its hoops, allowing beer to drain on to the floor and then into the ducks' feeding ditch,' said Steph. 'So her beloved birds were not dead at all but merely sleeping off the night before. Filled with remorse, she knitted waistcoats of Hawkshead yarn to keep them warm until their feathers were grown again.' Gorgeous.

Climb out of Haworth, home of all those Brontes, and after a mile or two you come to a pub on a lonely crossroads near the village of Stanbury – just as the hotly pursued Bonnie Prince Charlie did way back in the mid-eighteenth century. The Young Pretender stayed hidden there for a few weeks, relying on the tight-lipped locals to keep his whereabouts secret – albeit additionally persuaded by the threat of having their tongues cut out if they breathed a word.

Which is why the pub nowadays bears the unlikely name of the *Old Silent Inn*.

(When he was finally betrayed, Charlie rode out into the sunset, leaving a band of comrades to watch his back. A fierce battle ensued and one of his loyalists was killed. And you are quite likely to come across him today hanging around the bar, dressed in a long dark coat.)

And the pub is further immortalised in a best-selling detective thriller by American crime writer Martha Grimes – 'the Dorothy Sayers of the 1980s' according to the *New York Times* – entitled *The Old Silent* and featuring Superintendent Richard Jury, who just happened to be staying at the inn when someone got bumped off.

'I wouldn't trust any of the regulars nowadays to stay silent for any length of time about anything as juicy as that,' said smiling landlord Paul Stapleton. 'But they are a very well behaved bunch and very supportive of their local.'

It was snowing a blizzard when I slithered to a halt in the car park of the *Busby Stoop Inn*, a few miles outside Thirsk, in North Yorkshire, adding an even more sinister atmosphere to the grim events of 1702 that gave the pub its name.

After bumping off his father-in-law, a local chap called Tom Busby was hanged on the gallows that in those days stood just across the road from the inn and his ghost has been a frequent visitor to the inn ever since, with head drooping and the noose still around his head.

'A former landlord used to keep a stool free for him at the bar,' says current licensee Chris Rowley, 'but when he left he donated it to Thirsk Museum.'

And all you have to do when you get to the bar counter at the *Shroppie Fly*, on the banks of the Shropshire Union Canal at Audlem, is to look around you to begin to understand the origin of that most curious of pub names.

'Fly' boats were the high speed barges that used to ply the waterway, delivering the most important or perishable goods. Look at the bar and you realise it is made up of the colourfully painted bow and part of the oaken main body of the *Shroppie Fly*, a fine example of one of the elite craft once built thereabouts.

'Although we are very much a local pub, we get a huge number of boaties, many of whom come back year after year,' says landlady Kate Griffiths. 'Some of them even return to us by car to join in our Saturday night live music and the folk sessions we have every Monday.'

Nathaniel Bentley, an ironmonger in Leadenhall Street, in the City of London, was so distraught when his bride-to-be died on the eve of the great day that he locked up the room in which the wedding feast was to be held, never to enter it again. Emotionally destroyed, he never washed or changed clothes again and even allowed his cats to rot away wherever they breathed their last.

Everyone loves an eccentric, of course, and Nathaniel's business prospered, despite the pronounced pong of its surrounding. And when he finally retired in 1804, the landlord of the nearby *Old Port Wine Shop* in Bishopsgate, bought the room's contents lock, stock and barrel – including the odd decomposed cat – and put them on display in his pub, promptly renaming it *Dirty Dick's*.

Less well known, however, is the tale of how its metropolitan neighbour, the *Widow's Son*, in Bow, East London, came to be. A widow's seafaring son was due back to his cottage home on Good Friday, 1824, and sent word that what he hungered for most of all were hot-cross buns to celebrate his return.

Sadly he never made it home but his mourning mum never let a Good Friday go by without baking another bun which she added to the string hanging from a ceiling beam. In 1848 the cottage became a pub and successive landlords have ever since invited a Royal Navy sailor to add another bun to the ever hardening collection.

The foundations of *The Ostrich*, in Colnbrook, not far from Heathrow Airport, were laid in 1106, when Henry I was on the throne. Not too many ostriches have roamed that neck of the woods, either then or now, but that has not prevented generations of tap room punters improving on its original name – The *Hospice*!

(Anyway, The Hospice would scarcely have been an appropriate name for the premises presided over by its most infamous landlord, Jarman, back in the 17th Century, who enhanced his profits by murdering his more opulent-looking patrons after they had retired for the night. One room was ingeniously modified so that the bed could be tilted to decant the luckless sleeping customer through a trap door into a vat of boiling liquid beneath. Travel has long been a dangerous business.)

Charles I seldom passed a pub without popping in for a quickie and when he stopped to have his horse shod and discovered that Godmanstone in Dorset – horror of horrors – contained not one single pub he promptly granted a licence to the blacksmith so that he could provide him with the necessary refreshment. Not surprisingly, the *Smith's Arms* is today a leading contender for the title of smallest inn in Britain – so small that, when I visited, I was amused that they had to paint the name on an adjacent building. (Sadly the pub is currently closed for business – small, in this instance, proving less than beautiful.)

His adversary, Oliver Cromwell, although born in his grandfather's boozer, the wonderfully historic *George* in Huntingdon (of which more later), was a bit of a puritan in his drinking habits and not nearly as beneficial to the licensed trade. But when he stopped over at Newbridge, just west of Oxford, for a night's kip during the Civil War, he did choose an inn in which to lay his head.

While checking in, he noticed that the rose he wore on his tunic was decidedly wilted. The landlord enterprisingly summoned a pint of ale, into which he thrust the drooping flower, whereupon its petals sprang to life – hence *The Rose Revived*.

(Assistant manager, Vicky Leney, came up with two other theories when I called by. One, it was once called *The Rose*, had its name changed to *The Crown* and a later landlord chose to revert to its former name by calling it the *Rose Revived*. And two, when it was badly damaged by floods in the early 20th century, all that survived when it was rebuilt was a single rose bush. It's up to you, of course, but I know which version I prefer.)

And all those *Swan with Two Necks* up and down the land were never in reality such unlikely versions of Shakespeare's beloved feathered residents of the River Avon.

In Britain, swans have traditionally belonged to the reigning monarch but back in the 16th century Elizabeth I granted ownership of some to the Worshipful Company of Vintners. In order to identify those that had passed out of regal command into the licensed trade, they were marked with two notches, or nicks, on their beak.

By pub standards, the leap from nick to neck over the years was little more than a hop.

So much for the oddities – but how's about all those common or garden *Red Lions*, *Rose and Crowns* and the ubiquitous *Marquis of Granby*?

Let's begin with the dear old Marquis – for no other reason than if ever the Great British Pub feels the need to adopt a patron saint, here surely is their man.

John Manners, Marquis of Granby, commanded the entire British contingent of 32,000 troops in the Anglo-Hanoverian army that took on the French in the Seven Years War – galloping at the head of his soldiers in the hazardous but astonishingly successful cavalry charge at Warburg in 1760.

His courage during the campaign became legendary and his respect for the men under his command so intense that he bought a pub for every one of his non-commissioned officers who were injured and invalided out of the army, rather than see them starve under the derisory terms of their discharge.

He died £37,000 in debt, or about £4-million in today's money, but the first response of all his beneficiaries was to call their newly-acquired boozers after their beloved commander. (During his charge on Warburg his helmet flew off, revealing a premature absence of hair – so that's why whenever today we take on an objective against all the odds we 'go into it bald-headed.' Just thought you'd like to know that.)

The 55-years' life of the chap destined to become Charles II was a positive rollercoaster of ups and downs and never was he quite as desperately down as when he found himself up in a tree.

You know the story. When his father, Charles I, was unfortunate enough to lose his head back in 1649, his 19-year-old eldest son made a gallant if foolhardy attempt to regain the throne by taking over the royal resistance to Oliver Cromwell. But a couple of years later his ambitions came to a sticky end when his forces were crushed at Worcester and his attempt to flee into Wales was cut off by the enemy.

Seeking shelter at a good friend's pad, Boscobel House, in Staffordshire, he was obliged to dress up as a woodman and thereafter hide in the branches of a tree for a whole day as Cromwell's men continually passed beneath him. After that hairiest of escapes he hot-footed it to France.

Cromwell's Commonwealth government turned out to be a pretty dreary affair and when he died, the young Charles II was invited back to restore the monarchy with a hero's welcome in London on his 30th birthday. The story of his forest hideaway spread around the land like wildfire and the tree that gave him asylum became known and immortalised as the Royal Oak.

And all over the country, pubs – well used to having to curry favour for survival in changing times – rechristened themselves accordingly. Today, according to the British Beer and Pub

Association in a 2007 survey, the *Royal Oak* is Britain's second most popular pub sign, with more than 600 scattered around the land. (As with any other debate concerning pubs no one can totally agree – and why should they? Otherwise there would be no point in having pubs in the first place.}

And in first place? With rather more than 750 fellow creatures displayed on pub signs throughout Britain, our dear friend the *Red Lion* holds pride (excuse the pun) of place at No 1. Following the already accepted practice of showing total allegiance to the top man (or woman) of the time, many chose to take as their symbol the red lion that featured on the crest of John of Gaunt, founder in the 14th century of the House of Lancaster, which in turn provided England with kings Henry IV, Henry V and Henry VII.

But it was from north of the border that the real boost to its numbers sprang. When Elizabeth I died in 1603 without an heir, James VI of Scotland took on the additional job of being James I of England and immediately decreed that the national emblem of Scotland, the House of Stuart's red lion rampant, should be displayed on all public buildings throughout his united realm, which were deemed to include pubs.

But how on earth did the *White Hart*, with 427 boozers at the last count, make it into the bronze medal position? Blowed if I know. Richard II was cornered by a white deer (if it was a deer older than five that would have made him a hart) in Windsor Forest and famously rescued by a chap called Herne the Hunter, who died in the process. Whether that was why Richard had a white hart introduced into his coat of arms is uncertain and whether that was the source of a plethora of *White Hart* pubs all over the place is equally unsure.

Alternatively, in heraldry, the hart symbolises peace and harmony, the white adding purity into the equation. Peace? Harmony? Purity?... Pubs? I pass.)

Rose and Crown (326), *Kings Head* (310), *Kings Arms* (284), *Queens Head* (278) and *Crown* (261), bringing up the next five places in the Association's list and having dropped the odd apostrophe along the way, follow the same timeless policy of survival by flattery.

(In its own survey at precisely the same time, CAMRA also included *Red Lion, Royal Oak, Crown* and *White Hart* in its top ten but also put *Swan, Railway, Plough, White Horse, Bell* and *New Inn* up there as well. You pays your money...)

Both those surveys are a bit long in the tooth as we stride further into the second decade of the century, of course, and no one knows exactly how many lions, harts or bits of royal anatomy have since either been knocked down or turned into *Slug and Lettuces* or similar non-historical inanities.

But I am grateful to the *Mail on Sunday* magazine, *Live*, which commissioned a bang up-to-date survey (admittedly in England alone) from researcher and graphic designer, John Coates, and which will surely delight every statistician and number-cruncher among the drinking classes.

According to the admirable Coates, the *Red Lion* is still miles out in front but only with 518 swinging signs to its name. This is unsurprising because of the marque's Scottish ancestry and therefore the large number still to be found north of the border.

Thereafter, the *Crown* just edges the *Royal Oak* into second place (436 to 434) and the *White Hart* (320) and *White Horse* (300) complete the top five.

But other mind-blowing conversation-stoppers wait in the wings.

In the transport section, for example – and ignoring the *White Horse* with its limited capacity – the *Ship* (202) just edges out the *Railway* (192) with the *Coach & Horses* hanging on to third place with 147.

Apart from all those heraldic lions, horses and harts, the *Swan* (270) comfortably leads the animal department with the *Greyhound* (155), *Fox and Hounds* (143) and the similarly adversarial *Hare and Hounds* (138) vying for the places. But that's maybe a touch unfair on the bovine fraternity because if the *Bulls Head* (126) could patch it up with the *Bull* (123) it would leapfrog into second place.

Agriculturally, the *Wheatsheaf* and *Plough* are inseparable with 216 each but on the jobs front their gatherer and operator, the *Farmers* (49), trails the *Masons Arms* on a tantalising 99, with the

Blacksmiths (62), *Carpenters* (57), *Miners* (53), *Butchers* (52) and *Bricklayers* (51).

The *Cricketers*, with no fewer than 130 English pubs paying nominal allegiance to the noble cause, lead the sports category by a country mile but if the *Fishermans* (17) and *Anglers* (12) could only settle their differences they might just come into sight on the horizon.

Does it matter what a pub's called? You have to be joking. Not so long ago the Most Reverend Vincent Nichols, leader of the Catholic Church in England and Wales, was moved to write an indignant letter to the owners when their intention to change the name of *The Cardinal*, close to Westminster Cathedral, to the *Windsor Castle* became known.

It wasn't because he was hotly tipped to be made cardinal himself that fired the great man's wrath, apparently, but because the pub was named after a Cardinal Manning, who courageously supported the London dockers' strike way back in 1889.

And, with respect to the Most Rev and his Anglican oppo in Canterbury, has there ever been a motorist, or even a walker, who has been sent on his way with the counsel to turn right at Holy Trinity, bear left at St Michael and All Angels and watch out for the new roundabout just past St John the Evangelist?

If pubs didn't exist – or, worse still, changed their name – would any one of us ever get to wherever it was we were destined for?

Between rounds...

Pubs might change their names from time to time, but their patrons are traditionally loath to make any such change to their favoured drink therein. Indeed, their habits of a lifetime are usually so predictable that if they take more than a second or two to get from threshold to bar counter, their 'usual' is either awaiting them or at least well on its way.

So to change the drinking habits of an entire boozer – or at least a measurable chunk of it – is an achievement that anyone ought to be quite proud of. Ought to – so why does the memory invoke such painful pangs of guilt?

After a year or so in the Manchester office of the *Daily Mail* I was hauled down to Fleet Street to join an awesome team of veterans as a nervous incomer – only to find old and experienced heads shaking their heads in bewilderment.

An edict had gone out that anyone, regardless of stature, found incapacitated because of overindulgence in alcohol would be summarily dismissed. 'Pissed and you're out' seemed to be the unprecedented order of the day.

And that's when the thunderbolt struck its target.

J L (Jim) Manning, sports editor and probably the best known 'name' on the paper because of his highly entertaining weekly contribution to BBC Radio's *Sports Report*, was given his marching orders – apparently for no other reason than for wetting his whistle too enthusiastically too early.

The troops were dumbstruck. Two floors beneath the news room, the *White Swan* – or Mucky Duck as it was not too originally known throughout The Street – was the temporary home of so many reporters and photographers at any one time that the public phone in the saloon bar was actually connected to the *Mail* internal switchboard. There was even a typewriter on a shelf next to it which could be 'played' by a loyal colleague whenever an inmate found it necessary to ring home and explain how he was being kept late in the office. (Older readers might remember the satisfying ping when the typewriter approached the end of every line – evidence of fervent activity to any doubter's ears.) The pub and the daily office routine were intertwined and wholly dependent on each other. Was this the end of our world?

It was about that time that the great sherry houses of Jerez won a momentous High Court judgment that only they could call their product Sherry. Any interloper from outside Jerez, even elsewhere in Spain, had to attach the country of origin to the tipple on offer – British sherry, Cyprus sherry, Spanish sherry or whatever.

The overjoyed victors – Harvey's, Sandeman, Williams & Humbert, Gonzalez Byass and Domecq spring to mind – held a celebratory press conference to which I and notebook were despatched. Every interviewee in turn pressed a schooner of his nectar upon me which it would have been churlish, nay positively adversarial, to refuse. Some even insisted I compare the heavenly warmth of the *amontillado* with the untamed power of the *oloroso*.

Back in the Mucky Duck, notebook filled and still only a little past 1pm, I delivered the exciting news to my fellow hacks. 'Sherry is the answer!' I spluttered. 'Our problems are solved!'

And when none in the audience appeared to get hold of the significance of my news, I patiently explained that I had been obliged to down at least six schooners of the stuff and here I was, as sober as breakfast.

The resulting huddle assessed the claim, agreed that I appeared to be neither slurring nor slavering and when a close examination revealed no noticeable dilation of the eyeballs – we had all reported enough drink driving cases to know what to look for – within minutes Buck the landlord was combing his cellar for additional schooners as bottle after bottle of his rather meaner fortified wine from Cyprus flew off the shelf.

What Truman's, the brewery company that owned the *White Swan*, made of the sudden transformation of Buck's weekly order, I know not. Nor can I remember the exact duration of the Mucky Duck Sherry Period. But I am sure that songs of praise were being sung in Famagusta long before sanity returned to the pathways of EC4.

Only now, under the 40-year Fleet Street Secrets Act I've just invented, can the murky details of the rest of that momentous day be revealed.

After adding two or three sizeable dollops of Buck's Cyprus Surprise to the ambrosia of the morning I returned to my desk, flung my obligatory mac over an adjacent chair, carefully lined up a purple Roneo sheet behind the copy paper in my Remington Rand and prepared to type 'William Greaves' on the top left hand corner of the page. Disaster! No matter how clearly I recalled the correct spelling of my own name, a mysterious breakdown in the linkage system that connects brain to fingers meant that no single digit on either hand could move separately from the others. In other words, depressing the letter W activated an identical response from Q, E, R, and T.

My dear pal Dermot Purgavie once reported on the activities of a strange literary sect in the States that sought to outlaw the letter E by delivering his entire weekly column from America without once using that invaluable vowel. But even he would have been floored by having to use four adjacent letters simultaneously – even if the mechanics of the old-fashioned typewriter would have allowed such profligacy.

It was crisis time. Any pride in having accidentally stumbled upon Sherry Quaffer's Finger to add to the better known medical conditions of Housemaid's Knee and Athlete's Foot in much the same way that Alexander Fleming had earlier chanced upon Penicillin did naught to still a mounting wave of panic. Could the shortest ever Fleet Street career be already nearing its end?

Salvation, however, was miraculously at hand. The news editor and his deputy had chosen on this day not to share lunchtime refreshment with their flock but instead to attend a function elsewhere which was obviously and mercifully still going strong.

Clutching mac and notebook, I fled down the back stairs, made for the nearest telephone box and phoned in my piece without the copytaker once having to question my immaculate diction. And half an hour later I rang the news desk to tell them that I seemed to have picked up a bug and would it be all right if I went home to recover?

Within 24 hours I was able to confront a lightly boiled egg and a further 24 hours saw me back behind my desk.

The worst element of this shameful incident was, of course, the fact that I could not protect any of my colleagues from themselves falling foul of Sherry Quaffer's Finger. The merest whisper falling upon the ears of the powers-that-were would surely have resulted in my ignominious dismissal.

I had survived but I had to leave others to plough their own furrow. Many lessons had been learnt. High on the list was the indisputable fact that the Great British Pub, despite its fabled hospitality, can hold hidden and vengeful pitfalls if not treated with the respect it deserves.

And I've somehow got through the last four decades without a single sip of sherry.

Chapter ten

In words and pictures

He might have been technically awake for a few hours but for that greatest of all post-war journalists, Vincent Mulchrone, life began at 11am.

That was when the editor of the *Daily Mail* summoned all his department heads for the morning conference which would discuss the likely format of the following morning's paper and was also the moment, with the chiefs otherwise occupied, for the Indians to make for the pub.

It was a daily excursion known as the 'conference quickie' and for the reporters it meant a dash for the back stairs that led to the saloon bar of the *White Swan*.

But for we small band of self-important feature writers – 'poets corner' or 'the reporters with adjectives' – the destination was the tiny back bar of *The Harrow*.

Here we would be met by Len the barman who would have ready on the bar a glass of Fernet Branca (a grape-distilled spirit with added myrrh, rhubarb, chamomile, cardamon, aloa and saffron, recommended for the treatment of menstrual and gastrointestinal disorders, baby colic or, in this particular case, hangovers,) a glass of tap water and a half bottle of Champagne.

The morning ritual would be conducted in total silence. Vincent would walk to the bar, swig down the Fernet Branca, screw his face into a contortion of disgust, reach for the water, down it in one, shiver briefly and then take a heart-starting sip of the Rheims restorer at the very moment Len had expertly released the cork.

Only then would he have the strength or composure to acknowledge the rest of the company. 'Morning Len. Morning chaps...' Another day had begun.

The fact that only Vincent was paid enough to afford our morning bubbly and the rest of us were digging far too deeply into the family housekeeping was simply accepted as being an unavoidable sacrifice to the decent order of things. We were in the theatre of the master.

Of all the newspapermen I have been privileged to work alongside (or in opposition to, come to that) Vincent Mulchrone remains the only one who could honestly be described as a 'man of literature'. (Among the hundreds of unforgettable pieces to emerge from his typewriter, the most appropriate to recall in this place concerned a memorable community rescue act in Monaghan, Republic of Ireland, and contained one of the longest drop intros in Fleet Street legend – opening with *I do believe I am about to write what may be the most beautiful sentence in the English language* and some 500 words later revealing the contents of that treasured sentence: *The customers bought the pub.*

O joy!)

Alas, Vincent left us for the great newsroom in the sky many years ago but call into that same little snug today and not only does it declare itself to be The Mulchrone Bar but on the wall inside are displayed a smiling picture of the man himself alongside a glowing tribute from no less a figure than Associated Newspapers proprietor Lord Harmsworth. The journalists have long departed from Fleet Street – most returning only to say goodbye to former colleagues at their spiritual home of St Bride's Church – and whether the modern-day clientele of City folk spare a glance for the heritage of their surroundings, I know not, but every time I enter I hear the ghostly 'Morning Len, morning chaps' as clearly as t'were yesterday.

The chemical interaction between artistic genius and the Great British Pub has long been a recognised historical phenomenon but whether the pub spawned the inspiration of scribe or artist or the writer or artist merely graced the boozer of his or her choosing is a matter for conjecture. Certainly in Vincent's case, as with a whole generation of Fleet Street supremos, more ideas emerged from pub conversation than from any other source. Perhaps the word and the glass were merely happily married.

 As was certainly the case within the Rabbit Room of the *Eagle and Child* in St Giles', Oxford, during the 1930s and 1940s when every Tuesday morning a fly on the wall would have been privileged to eavesdrop upon J R R Tolkien, C S Lewis and other members of a literary circle of Oxford University students and dons known as The Inklings when they took their regular seats in the pub they affectionately knew as the *Bird and Baby* or more often simply the *Bird* to chat about sundry elves, Hobbits, orcs and other residents of Middle Earth and more distant planets and read latest extracts from their books-to-be.

Such meeting were not without their moments of good natured dissention and on one occasion when Tolkien was in mid-story, Lewis was famously heard to mutter 'Oh, no, not another fucking elf!' But it is also widely acknowledged that it was only Lewis's enthusiasm for his fellow academic's imagination at these weekly pub get-togethers that persuaded Tolkien to press on with his now famous trilogy, *The Hobbit, Lord of the Rings* and *The Silmarillion.*

And a framed hand-written letter addressed to the landlord and signed by all the Inklings, thanking him for the excellence of the ham they had just eaten, still hangs on the Rabbit Room wall. It is dated 1948 – the year Lewis completed the first draft of *The Lion, the Witch and the Wardrobe.* (Nowadays, the pub is still the narrow zigzag of nooks and crannies that those distinguished regulars would have known and the food is still as mouth-wateringly simple, dominated by a daily variety of home-made pies. The day I walked in the notice on the wall proudly proclaimed: 'Last week we sold 2,481 pints of ale and 369 pies' – a true feast for Hobbits.)

'As well as present day Oxford students, tourists come here in their thousands because the literary history of the pub is well-known everywhere,' says manager Kerry Skrzypiec, who is no stranger to entertaining literary pilgrims. 'My previous pub was the *Crown,* just down the road in Cornmarket, where William Shakespeare was a regular visitor and was apparently having an affair with Mrs Davenant, wife of the landlord, John Davenant.' Indeed, it is widely rumoured that the Bard was the father of her son, William – later, Sir William Davenant and himself a playwright. The time-honoured relationship between literary prowess and the Great British Pub could scarcely get any closer than that.

And would there ever have been a Robinson Crusoe if Daniel Defoe had not struck up a casual conversation with one Alexander Selkirk over a pint of best in the *Llandoger Trow* pub in downtown Bristol? Come to that, would we ever have learnt of the adventures of Jim Hawkins if that very same pub – renamed the *Admiral Benbow* in one of the world's best loved stories of derring do – had not become Robert Louis Stevenson's model for Jim's family home in *Treasure Island?*

L S Lowry, that magnificent painter of industrial life with its 'matchstalk men and matchstalk cats and dogs', as the hit song of yesteryear so memorably described them, is not only revered as a one-time regular at his favourite Manchester pub, *Sam's Chop House*, but is still to be seen propping up his corner of the bar. To be more precise, since he died back in 1976, a life-size bronze statue of the great man now sits on his former stool.

He would pop in of a lunchtime for a half pint of beer and a bowl of soup from his studio in nearby Pall Mall – exactly as I did (only forget the soup and multiply the half pint several times) from the equally adjacent offices of the *Manchester Evening News*. But we never met. Dammit.

Current owner Roger Ward, says he got the idea of commissioning the statue from sculptor Peter Hodgkinson when he came across a picture of Lowry fast asleep on a chair in the pub painted by his now hugely sought-after student, Harold Riley.

(Now, Harold I *do* know. Lovely man, he told me recently how he once declined to paint a portrait of former Malta Prime Minister Dom Mintoff, because of lack of time and how customs officials at the airport later sought to confiscate his sketch pad on the spurious grounds that he had no work permit. Riley, bless him, refused to hand it over and instead tore it to shreds in front of the opportunist officer's astonished eyes. Lowry, obdurate Lancastrian, obviously taught his protégé more than mere painting technique.)

First-time visitors to the *Tower Bank Arms*, a simple and charming pub in the heart of the Lake District in Near Sawrey, not far from the banks of Lake Windermere, might well feel certain they'd seen it somewhere before. And they would be right...

Pick up your copy of Beatrix Potter's *The Tale of Jemima Puddle-Duck* and you will read how Kep, the wise old collie dog, 'trotted down the village to look for two foxhound puppies who were out at walk with the butcher.' And, sure enough, there they are on the opposite page, pictured in the author's unmistakeable brush strokes, outside the Tower Bank pub.

It was a little ahead of opening time when I bowled up out of a snow blizzard but, in the absence of any promenading foxhounds, current landlord Anthony Hutton, true to age-old rustic traditions of courtesy, opened the door with a welcoming 'Best come in and I'll make you a cup of coffee.'

And in no time at all he was talking affectionately about his former famous near-neighbour and how she wasn't much into pubs – and didn't have much time for children either. 'I'm afraid she was rather deprived of her own childhood and was perhaps a bit resentful about that,' he told me.

And elderly neighbour Willow Taylor well remembers the many times as a little girl she was honoured to be at the receiving end of the wonderful storyteller's disapproving turn of phrase. 'Our playground in those days was the main road that ran through the village past the inn,' she recalls. 'On many occasions when we were playing cricket, rounders or tennis our ball would be knocked over the wall into Post Office Meadow, the field opposite Hilltop (BP's home) and owned by Beatrix Potter. Invariably, I would be the one climbing the wall to retrieve the ball just as she was coming along. "Why can't you use the gate? – You are a naughty little girl!" she would say.'

Without too many chimney pots nearby, the lovely little pub today is largely reliant on Beatrix Potter hunters for survival. 'But we keep our prices as low as we can and often when people come once they return year after year,' says Hutton.

Heaven knows how many pints were consumed, or how many literary thoughts hatched, by my old friend Laurie Lee in that wonderful Cotswold pub, the *Woolpack* in Slad. Did the eponymous heroine of Cider with Rosie, ever sit beside him there? Yes.

(Laurie once watched me going out to bat at the lovely neighbouring cricket ground at Sheepscombe and said to my wife, Suzanne: 'Bill is getting more like an ancient treasure as the years go by, don't you think? – a sort of silver-haired cathedral window.' Most of us don't talk like that. But what many people thereabouts didn't know was that the lovely Laurie had bought the land from a local farmer in order to guarantee the cricket club's survival.)

Pubs throughout the land proudly rejoice in their close association with the written word. Both local lad William Wordsworth and his frequent guest Sir Walter Scott spent happy hours in the *Swan* at Grasmere – Wordsworth even making affectionate mention of it in his poem *The Waggoners* – the *Black Bull* in Haworth, West Yorkshire, will be forever associated with the entire Bronte family.

While gainfully employed at the *Times* in Wapping, a sunny day would often tempt me down the road to Limehouse for a lunchtime jar or two at the *Grapes*, whose narrow and snug interior leads out on to magnificent shaded views along the Thames. And nor was I alone in this enjoyment. Charles Dickens was a regular visitor and immortalised it as the *Six Jolly Fellowship Porters* in *Our Mutual Friend*. Part of its attraction was nostalgic, however, because this was where he would often be made to stand on a table as a child and sing to the customers in the bar, the walls of which still abound in sketches of his many characters.

And on his travels, the great man relied heavily upon the researches made during his frequent visits to the *Ancient Unicorn* in Bowes, County Durham, for the creation of both Dotheby's Hall and its cruel headmaster Wackford Squeers in *Nicholas Nickleby*.

Frank Muir, the amiable genius behind so many hilarious television scripts was not only born in his grandfather's pub, the

Derby Arms in Ramsgate, but reputedly tried out his first joke in the bar there – at the age of six.

Visitors to Cornwall's most famous hostelry, *Jamaica Inn* at Bolventor, are positively inundated by memorabilia connected with Daphne du Maurier and her family and Jerome K Jerome not only stayed in the *Barley Mow* in Clifton Hampden, Oxfordshire, but also wrote much of his wonderful *Three Men in a Boat* while enjoying its hospitality.

And the beloved *Oxford Bar*, in Young Street, Edinburgh, is unique in that it remains the local of both Detective Inspector John Rebus and his real life creator, the bestselling Scottish author, Ian Rankin. Not only that but the medical team of Professor John Gates and Dr John Curt, who descend on the gruesome remains of Rankin's murder victims, just happen to have names that coincide with former owner of the 'Ox' John Gates, and teacher, regular Ox customer and personal pal, John Curt.

Current proprietor, Harry Cohen turns out to be a particularly jolly sort of chap – a tad surprising in view of the regular appearances of 'Harry Curran, the grumpiest barman in the world' in the Rebus books. ('Maybe I've cheered up now that I don't have to work for anyone,' says Harry.)

Among other regular Ox customers are Dr Andrew Tod, teacher and author of the successful *Memoirs of a Highland Lady* series of books and journalist and broadcaster Muriel Gray, who presented her popular hill walking series for Scottish Television not from her alleged hideaway high in the towering Munro Hills but from an upstairs bar in the Ox 'getting feisty with the regulars'.

The village of Winsford, at the meeting point of the rivers Winn and Exe in Somerset, is as lovely an example of picture postcard Britain as anyone would care to clap eyes on and at its hub lies the thatched *Royal Oak Inn*. Yet it was here, amid scrubbed tables, beamed bar and roaring fire, that the infamous highwayman Tom Faggus used to pop in on a regular basis to rob the inn's punters.

And another regular, mercifully at a different time, was doubtless the author Richard Doddridge Blackmore, who gratefully incorporated Faggus into his classic novel, *Lorna Doone*. (Modern visitors are greeted at the entrance with the notice: 'Muddy Paws Welcome' – hurrah!)

There are pubs that have entertained the literati in their times of leisure and there are those in which the wordsmiths have actually taken pen and ink to compose their magic prose while perched upon a bar stool, but there is probably only one pub that one of the most nationally adored poets has actually written *upon*.

Pass through the lounge bar (then the stables in which he would have tied up his horse) and the lovely snug (then the tackle room that would have received his saddle) and climb the stairs to one of the bedrooms of the *Globe Inn*, Dumfries, and you will find etched into one of the window panes, with his own diamond ring, a poem inscribed by Robbie Burns and intended for the eyes of a favourite young lady:

> *O lovely Polly Stewart*
> *O charming Polly Stewart*
> *There's not a flower that blooms in May*
> *That's half so fair as thou art.*

And upon a neighbouring pane, similarly etched, can still be seen a modified version of a more familiar refrain:

> *Gin a body meet a body*
> *Coming through the grain*
> *Gin a body kiss a body*
> *The thing's a body's ain.*

There was the occasion, too, When Burns, who described the *Globe* as his very favourite' howff' (or haunt), forgot to warn guv'nors Jock and Meg Hyslop of his and his companion's coming but was nonetheless provided with the sheep's head that their hosts had intended for themselves. Full of gratitude and a tinge of remorse, their beloved guest was prevailed upon to pronounce grace:

O Lord when hunger pinches sore,
Do thou stand us in stead,
And send us, from thy bounteous store,
A tup or wether head!
    O, Lord since we have feasted thus,
Which we so little merit,
Let Meg take away the flesh,
And Jock bring in the spirit!
Now there speaks a truly satisfied customer.

Chapter eleven

Unreal ale

Back in its early days when the TV soap *Emmerdale Farm* was filmed in gloriously unspoilt Lyttondale in the Yorkshire Dales, the locals got so fed up with the swelling army of gawking camera-clickers who invaded their tranquillity by the coachload that they pleaded with Yorkshire Television to take its cameras elsewhere.

The company duly obliged and, under cover of darkness and oath of secrecy, switched its allegiance to the village of Esholt, so close to the cities of Leeds and Bradford that its producers erroneously believed that the soap's groupies would never think to seek their rustic idols in such a near-urban hideaway.

How wrong they were. In short time, a field had to be concreted to accommodate the coaches and the cameras of the voyeurs clicked anew.

This time, however, the locals rather enjoyed their new-found fame. The village pub, mundanely christened the *Commercial*, which one day every week had its sign and name covered up to pronounce itself the *Woolpack*, enjoyed galloping custom and the local post office/corner shop did a roaring trade with its Emmerdale diaries, Emmerdale crayons, Emmerdale notelets and Emmerdale everything-elses.

Despatched to the scene with a photographer to report for the *Daily Mail* on the latest fictional TV-inspired invasion, we were momentarily thrown by this lack of native resistance. Until, that is, we ventured out of the village centre in search of the soap's eponymous epicentre.

And, glory of glories, there at the advent of a lengthy driveway was a large hand-written sign which remains in the mind's eye to this day: THIS IS NOT EMMERDALE FARM – F*** OFF!

(The besieged farmer, who apparently had no asterisks at his disposal, apologised for his unequivocal language when we bravely disregarded his unambiguous instructions and ventured to his door, but said that he was several weeks late getting in his previous autumn's harvest because of the multitudes invading his land and that the 'real' Emmerdale Farm was several miles away.)

But the village pub has now gladly given up any doubts about its role as an icon of the silver screen and renamed itself *The Woolpack* for all seven days of the week.

It was back in 1976 when the pub played host to the Emmerdale squad for the first time and, in fairness, it wasn't Yorkshire TV that gave the game away but a rather unthinking Bradford Tourist Board that chose a picture of the *Commercial* for the front cover of its brochure – a picture instantly recognised by the soap's legion of aficionados.

After stints by Amos Brearly and Henry Wilks, Alan Turner became the new landlord in the world of make belief in January 1991, with grandiose ideas of taking it upmarket, changing the brewery and holding a spectacular re-opening in the revealing presence of Miss Skipdale Breweries – with a consequent surge in real life customers.

And although the programme, which dropped the 'Farm' from its title in 1989, has not been filmed in the village since 1997 – when a brand new set was built in the grounds of nearby Harewood House – the current boss reckons that at least fifty per cent of her trade during the summer months is made up of the Emmerdale faithful.

And the Woolpack remains unique among soap pubs in that it actually exists. The *Rovers Return Inn* and the *Queen Victoria* in Albert Square have only ever been studio creations and the *Bull* in Ambridge, although inspired by a real boozer in which I recently enjoyed a couple of excellent pints, is really as non-existent as Ambridge and the family Archer themselves.

For a mere figment of the imagination, however, the history of the *Rover's Return Inn* is probably better chronicled than any other pub in the land. Its first two landlords, Jim Cobishley (1902 – 1919) and George Diggins (1919 – 1937), although now formerly listed on the honours board, were actually long gone and buried before *Coronation Street* was ever dreamed up as the working-class saga it has become and even that unforgettable duo, Jack and Annie Walker, had been in charge for a full 23 years before their debut on screen in December, 1960.

When Annie finally retired in 1984, their wayward son Billy held the reins for less than a year until the pub's most popular barmaid, Bet Lynch, became manager to her great surprise for ten action-packed years. After them in fairly quick succession came Jack and Vera Duckworth, Natalie Barnes, Fred Elliott, Mike Baldwin and Duggie Ferguson (between 2001 and 2006) and then Steve and Liz McDonald from thereon.

And few pubs in the land can possibly have experienced so many memorable moments that have punctuated the years. Remember Martha Longhurst's death in the snug (with Violet Carson, sorry Ena Sharples, bravely playing *Down at the Old Bull and Bush* on the piano to hide her tears), the lorry crash outside that was thought to have killed Deirdrie Langton's baby in her pram until it was discovered that someone had abducted her a few moments earlier (1979) and the 1986 fire that so rearranged the inner structure of the building and which almost choked Bet to death in her bedroom – actress Julie Goodyear's nightdress really did catch fire during the filming, so her scream was entirely genuine.

No, there was never a dull moment down at the *Rover's Return*.

Television ratings are ruthless slavedrivers, however, and if the *Rovers* can boast one inferno, its opposite number, the *Queen Victoria*, in Albert Square, watering hole for all those *Eastenders*, has already notched up two in a televised existence a full quarter century less than its northern rival.

The first conflagration was when Grant Mitchell, husband of freeholder Sharon Watts – remember her, daughter of Angie and 'Dirty' Den? – set fire to the place in an insurance scam in 1992 but the second, much more recently, was a far mightier affair, when the *Vic* actually had to be moved lock, stock and barrel to a specialist fire stage at Elstree Film Studios and the blaze involved 45 crew members, including make-up, a stunt team, fire safety officers, cameras, lighting, sound and costume departments.

Fires in real life boozers usually require far fewer personnel – even though sadly a couple of all-powerful soda siphons that used to do the trick are nowadays notably absent from the bar counter.

The *Bull's* starring role in more than 16,000 episodes of *The Archers* has received no finer accolade than when it was named Best Pub of Borsetshire in 2005.

But the real-life pub on which it is based needs no such transitory compliments – the *Old Bull* on the village green in Inkberrow, Hereford and Worcester, is a wonderful and welcoming Tudor-timbered hostelry with much more to its name than the wall full of signed pictures of the stars who have illumined that 'everyday story of countryfolk' these last sixty years.

After all, it was here that William Shakespeare lodged on his way to collect his wedding licence. 'And I've been told that Charles II's horse is buried under the very chair that you are sitting,' said landlady Lyn Fishburn, rather unexpectedly.

So that must have been back in 1651, when the king was fleeing from defeat at the Battle of Worcester which finally brought to an end the English Civil War.

I don't know exactly how many pubs there were in England during the 17th century but its a fair guess that either Charles I or his lad, Charles II, had a pint or two in all of them, even if both father and son had frequently to gulp the second one down pretty quickly when Oliver Cromwell's pursuing hordes came crashing over the horizon.

At least the unscheduled arrival of a regiment of fully-armed soldiers and neighing horses is something that not even desperate scriptwriters have thus far imposed on the management and punters of the *Rover's Return*, the *Queen Victoria*, the *Woolpack* and the *Bull* in Ambridge.

Chapter twelve

Those were the days

Let me tell you how I first became a temporary regular at that most famous of music hall pubs, the *Old Bull & Bush*.

Transferred for a few months' trial from the *Daily Mail* reporters' room in Manchester to the dizzy heights of Fleet Street, I was delighted to take up my dear friend George's gracious offer to share his flat on the third floor of a mansion block in Finchley Road.

Leaving wife and three small children back home in Derbyshire for the experimental period and thus plunged into such major domestic decisions as what to do about my limited stock of shirts and smalls, I quickly found a friendly launderette in nearby Golders Green.

And equally speedily adopted the weekly routine: clothes into washing machine, a quick drive up to the *Bull & Bush*, two pints, back to launderette, transfer clothes to dryer, one further pint up the road, collect clothes and mission accomplished.

But the timing could be critical. Quite early in the story I returned, two pints thoroughly enjoyed, to find a newly-arrived woman customer impatiently surveying a phalanx of washing machines, none of which was available. One machine had stopped, however, with the contents still within.

The newly arrived customer hesitated not. She deposited the cleansed clothes on to the floor and replaced them with her own; whereupon the discarded clothes' owner returned, slightly out of breath, to see her undies strewn around the premises for all to see. To my great surprise it was the very same lady with whom I had just been enjoying a pleasant chat over the second of my two pints up the road. With a surge of remorse, I realised that I could have been responsible for her late appearance.

The fight that ensued is forever carved into the memory. Long before the end of it the modesty of both combatants had been decidedly compromised by the total or partial demolition of most of their outer garments and blood flowed from a multitude of scratches, erotically distributed around acres of newly-exposed flesh. A small but enthusiastic audience stood mesmerised, occasionally applauding a particularly telling blow, and at the end of it all I found it necessary to depart from normal procedure and return to the *Bull & Bush* for a couple of further settlers. I had certainly not expected to meet up again with my new-found acquaintance so soon – or, come to that, so much of her so soon – and London was obviously going to prove more exciting than the wilds of Derbyshire's Peak District.

As well as being the subject of one of the best known songs of the Edwardian music hall age, the *Old Bull & Bush*, whose licence to sell ale dates back to 1721, has been the haunt of generations of artists including William Hogarth. And so it is just one of hundreds of pubs throughout Britain that can genuinely describe itself as historic.

Indeed, there are few better ways to brush up on British architectural and historical heritage – including that most elusive element of every child's schooldays, the dates of our kings and queens – than to embark on a major national pub crawl.

Pop in to the *Old Mint*, in Southam, Warwickshire, for example, and you can still see in the stone surrounds of the doorway the grooves made by Charles I's surviving soldiers as they sharpened their swords after the Battle of Edgehill in 1642 while awaiting payment for their services. (They had to hang around for some time because their monarch ordered his local nobles to bring in their silver to be melted down and made into coin of the realm – a handy resource if you happened to be a king.)

On the walls licensee Ben Barrett has assembled a bloodthirsty collection of weapons that would have been all too familiar to those early customers, the mullioned windows bear witness to the tavern's antiquity and today 'a steady stream of regulars just about keeps my head above water,' he says. Good news.

Even closer to the conflict, in the village of Edge Hill itself, stands the remarkable *Castle Inn*, complete with castellated tower, which was actually built a hundred years after that momentous conflict as a folly – brainchild of Sanderson Miller, gentleman architect and amateur pioneer of the Gothic revival during the Georgian period.

'Although it is a folly, it stands on the very site where Charles rallied his troops before marching down to the plain below,' says licensee Tom Douglas.

To unlock the portcullis and ascend the tower to one of the inn's three bedrooms and to gaze through the morning mist upon the battlefield hundreds of feet below, it is easy to imagine the sound of trumpets and the stench of death as 30,000 troops fought out the first bloody but indecisive battle of a civil war that was destined to last another four years.

'There are only about twenty houses in the village but we have a local butcher and the food brings people in from quite a few neighbouring villages,' says Tom's wife, Gill. 'And the view from the garden brings in customers in their hundreds during the summer months.'

The *Castle Inn* in Lydford, Devon, has presided over 500 years of local community life, including the harsh times when the village held regular court hearings against those who were alleged to have transgressed against the ancient stannary laws – often paying with their lives. As 17th century local poet William Browne recalled:

> *I oft have heard of Lydford Law;*
> *How in the morning they hang and draw*
> *– And sit in judgement after.*

But current landlord David Moxham, prefers the much later but ominously prophetic words of Anglo-French poet and writer

Hilaire Belloc, frequently thrusting a yellowing cutting before the unprotesting eyes of his regulars:

> *When you've lost your inns, drown your empty selves – because you will have lost the last of England.*

And he proudly displays on the walls two 1,000AD silver pennies bearing the head of Ethelred the Unready, minted in the village, which would then have been more than enough to buy a couple of sheep. Now there's history for you.

Although pubs and court rooms nowadays have little in common – except that the former often is chosen as the restorative bolt hole for anyone recently subjected to the mental torment of the latter – time was when they frequently shared the same premises. The law and a pint or two strode arm in arm.

At the *Speech House*, a glorious old inn in the very heart of the Forest of Dean in Gloucestershire, there used even to be the wherewithal to carry out instant execution of anyone deemed to have offended against the laws of the forest. (Today's regulars might be a little apprehensive to learn that the inn's authority to carry out the death sentence has never been rescinded in the statutes of British law – although, in truth, inability to pay for the last pint might struggle to qualify for the ultimate penalty.)

The Verderer's Court, set up in the 17th century to settle disputes between iron founders and foresters and other local issues, still meets every three months in what is now the inn's dining room and the magistrates' bench remains exactly as it was more than three hundred years ago.

And more recent history is represented by the shovels used by the Queen and Prince Philip to plant a pair of oak trees opposite the front door on April 24, 1957, and a plaque in the grounds in memory of Sergeant Pilot D E Prior at the very spot where his Westland Whirlwind crashed on December 14, 1941.

But new owners Peter and Gill Hands are determined that the *Speech House* stays not only an hotel and a monument to history but also a 21st century pub. 'It used to be where the local workers met for a pint and we are here to make sure that it is returned to the community. We are just custodians – we come and we move on.'

Bravo!

Another pub that today looks back on its days as a seat of justice is the *White Bull* in Ribchester, Lancashire, a magnificent 17th century edifice complete with its original porch, supported by four Tuscan columns that were once part of a far older Roman fort nearby.

Not only did the pub double as the local court house back in the 18th century but one of its rooms acted as a holding cell – evidenced by a pair of leg irons firmly attached to the wall.

The Rose and Crown is one of Yorkshire's oldest inns, rightly acclaimed for both convivial hospitality and food – although its three bars and its dining room are separated by a labyrinth of corridors. Overlooking Bainbridge village green and dwarfed by the mountains of upper Wensleydale, it is hard to imagine that hundreds of years ago it was surrounded by dense forest – so dense that every evening a horn would be blown to guide the foresters back to their home.

Although these days no such guidance is necessary to locate the sanctuary of the *Rose and Crown*, the horn can still be found hanging on the wall by reception – a constant reminder of dim and distant days.

Duck your way into the *Church House Inn* in Rattery, Devon, and the first thing you spot is a list of vicars of the church next door, going back to Jeffery Hurning, 1139, followed by Walter de Pembroke in 1238 and Thomas Ballard who took over in 1260, with current incumbent David Winnington-Ingram in fiftieth spot.

'But actually this building goes back even a year further than the church because in those days they built a hostel for the workers who then set about building the church,' explained Ray Hardy, licensee these past nine years.

And rather more recent history comes in the form of a genuine notice on the wall offering fifty guineas reward for information leading to the '*discovery and apprehension of Thomas Carter alias*

Captain Black for his barbarous and inhuman attack on the Exeter Coach in October 1779 – a felon espied of late in the parlour of the Church House Inn, Rattery.'

(Another sign of rather more dubious authenticity outlines pub rules: *No Thieves, Fakirs, Rogues or tinkers – No Skulking Loafers or Flea-bitten Tramps.*)

And spare a thought for the luckless William Huskisson, MP for Liverpool, President of the Board of Trade and regular inhabitant at the bar of the charismatic *Farmers Arms* pub in Birtsmorton, Hereford and Worcester, who became the first man in the world to be killed by a passenger train – pulled by Stephenson's *Rocket*, no less – when all he was trying to do was open the Liverpool and Manchester Railway in 1830.

Now, there is history for you.

Chapter thirteen

The history makers

The *Swan Inn* first opened its doors to the villagers of Fittleworth, West Sussex, in 1382, the year after Wat Tyler led the Peasants' Revolt during the unpopular reign of the Black Prince's son, Richard II, and to walk through its friendly portals today and buy yourself a pint is to feel at first hand the awesome power of the Great British Pub.

But the *Swan's* fame has nothing to do with Dickie Two. And waste no time searching for the names of Rudyard Kipling, Diana Dors and Lady Hamilton in the visitors' book – although they are all in there somewhere. No, this delightfully olde worlde pub has hosted a far greater moment of history than any such transitory visits.

For it is here, one day in 1924, that Bert Temple, silk merchant thereabouts, founded the Ancient Order of Froth Blowers.

Froth blowers? Pause before ye mock.

OK, so it was dreamed up as a joke – with heartfelt charitable intentions – 'to foster the noble art and gentle and healthy pastime of froth blowing amongst gentlemen of leisure and ex-soldiers'. But within seven years it had captivated the nation, with an astonishing 700,000 members producing today's equivalent of more than £4.5 million to endow hospital cots and to fund holidays for thousands of needy children in the East End of London.

The good Mr Temple, forever grateful to Sir Alfred Fripp, whose stomach surgery had saved his life, sought to raise a mere £100 to support his saviour's children's charity by asking five shillings to become a member of his new-formed society – motto *Lubrication in Moderation* – which entitled the duly enrolled to blow froth off any fellow member's pint pot 'and occasionally off non-members' beer provided they are not looking or are of a peaceful disposition'.

The idea was to get new recruits to meet in pubs and clubs throughout Britain to enjoy 'beer, beef and baccy' and there to be fined for major sins, such as failure to wear the club's cufflinks – all fines and membership fees to be sent to Sir Alfred and Lady Fripp for their *Wee Waifs'* East End charity.

In late 1925 the *Sporting Times* started publishing articles on the Order's gatherings and the now-retired royal surgeon Fripp travelled the length and breadth of the land to recruit men (blowers), women (fairy belles) and their dogs (faithful bow-wows). Those who enrolled others received titles such as Blaster (twenty-five new members recruited), Tornado (100)... right up to Grand Typhoon (1,000).

The Order's marching song, a specially commissioned adaptation of *O du lieber Augustin,* became an overnight chart topper:

> *The more we are together, together, together*
> *The more we are together*
> *The merrier we'll be.*
> *For your friends are my friends*
> *And my friends are your friends*
> *And the more we are together*
> *The merrier we'll be.*

The order was voluntarily wound up in 1931 after the death of both Fripp and Bert Temple but not before the anti-liquor fraternity had been moved to a state of moralistic apoplexy and the emergence of a massive movement for the wellbeing of the deprived had proved for all time the national persuasiveness of the Great British Pub.

Pubs that have been around for long enough to be part of British heritage are one thing but pubs that have themselves *made* history are something else entirely.

(Not, of course, in the same league, but back in the late 1960s I started an annual gentlemen's cake-making competition in the *Red Lion,* a charming local in the village of Coleshill, Buckinghamshire, where entrants had to bring with them a signed affidavit from their 'other halves' that no help had been provided at the marketing, cooking or washing-up stage and any cake failing to make £10 at the subsequent auction had to be bought by its creator for at least that figure. Twenty years later the competition was revived, with widespread newspaper recognition, to raise money for my own *Capital Kids Cricket* charity, designed to reintroduce and maintain the great game in London's thousand-plus state schools, with the rather thin excuse that men who yearned to wield their willow on the village green of a Saturday afternoon had to be taught how to create their own cricket teas if a threatened rebellion by the country's much-presumed-upon cricket widows ever came to fruition. Who knows, one day we might yet have a nation of gentlemen cake-makers. That revival took place in the magnificent Marquess Tavern, in Islington, North London, whose sumptuous elegance once inspired a CAMRA reviewer to compare it with the interior of a Turkish brothel – clearly a more experienced traveller than most of its present day regulars.)

Anyway, back to the history makers.

Just imagine rolling home from a lunchtime session at the *Eagle*, in Cambridge, to have the wife challenge you with the traditional spousal enquiry: 'Well, what have you learnt at the pub today?' and being able to tell her how a couple of chaps wandered into the saloon and one of them blurted out 'We have discovered the secret of life.' Then being smugly able to pre-empt her response with: 'And, no dear... that was before they'd taken the head off their first pint.'

For that would have been the monumental occasion of February 28, 1953, when a couple of local boffins, Francis Crick and James Watson, bobbed in to announce to an astonished gathering of locals that they had just discovered this thing called DNA.

Wow!

(Mark you, the *Eagle* had a knack when it came to making history. Wander in today and you can still see the bar ceiling on which RAF pilots from all over the world forgathered to sign their names using only cigarette lighters, candles or lipstick during a reunion immediately after the end of World War Two.)

It's only a few minutes walk along the cobbled streets between converted Thames-side wharves that divide two of London's most famous pubs, the *Prospect of Whitby* and the *Town of Ramsgate*, but just imagine being a bystander on the day when the infamous Judge Jeffreys made a dash from one to the other before spending his dying days incarcerated in the Tower of London.

The *Prospect of Whitby* has a flagstone floor dating right back to the pub's origin in 1543; its bar is a rare pewter top built over barrels and from its small balcony at the rear you can listen to the rhythmic lapping of the waters of the Thames beneath.

But it was none of those features that drew the notorious Jeffreys to become one of its most regular customers. The 'Hanging Judge' had delighted in sentencing to death all 200 men and their leaders after the failed attempt by the Monmouth Rebellion of 1685 to overthrow the Catholic King James II. Later he was there to take even greater pleasure in witnessing the appallingly stretched out death of each and every one of his victims as they were tied to a post, near-drowned by successive risings of the tide and finally garrotted at Execution Dock, a few hundred yards upstream.

After the king fled to France, Jeffreys was found hiding in a coal cellar at the pub and just had time to flee to the nearby *Town of Ramsgate*, where he gulped down his very last pint before being dragged off to the Tower.

The *Town of Ramsgate* almost certainly dates back even further to the 1460s and the Wars of the Roses, becoming known as the *Red Cow* in 1533 – a rather ungallant reference to a particularly sharp-tongued redheaded barmaid of the time – before earning its present name from the fishermen of Ramsgate who refused to pay tax for landing their catch at Billingsgate market and offloaded it instead at Wapping New Stairs, immediately alongside the pub. Nowadays its long narrow bar leads from Wapping High Street to a small terrace overlooking the river and landlady Janet Biddle is a woman with a purpose.

'We've got a plaque on the wall presented by CAMRA because of our place in history as the last drinking place of Judge Jeffreys. We do get lots of tourists at weekends but we belong to our regulars. We have no separate restaurant and the only food we serve is bangers and mash, pies and simple fare like that – we're a pub, and determined to keep it that way.' Well done, Janet.

No fewer than seven past kings of England have laid their head overnight on the pillows of The *Angel and Royal*, Grantham, Lincolnshire, but the day it forever planted its name in the annals of history was when Richard III signed the death warrant for the Duke of Buckingham in its dining room.

THE CLISSOLD ARMS

Ray and Dave Davies, founder members of The Kinks, played their first gig in the *Clissold Arms*, Fortis Green, London, in 1957 and no serious fan will be unfamiliar with those immortal lines in their subsequent hit *Fortis Green*:

> *Mum would shout and scream when Dad would come home drunk.*
> *When she'd ask him where he'd been, he said 'up the Clissold Arms'*
> *Chattin' up some hussy, but he didn't mean no harm.*

While on the subject, don't forget that it was in the *Star Inn*, Guildford, that The Stranglers (then called the Guildford Stranglers) gave their first performance in 1974.

And *King Tut's Wah Wah Hut* in Glasgow might not sound like a pub, although pub it certainly is, but it was here that Manchester duo Oasis was first spotted and signed up in 1993, Blur, Pulp, Radiohead and Glasgow's own Travis all played there before or after they hit the big time and the Manic Street Preachers once told a live festival audience that Tut's was the first venue that ever offered them a hot meal on tour...

Those of us old enough to remember the morning of June 2, 1953, when the morning papers had belatedly been forced to split their front page coverage between that day's coronation of Queen

Elizabeth II (which the whole country was preparing to celebrate) and probably the greatest news story of the decade – the ascent of Mount Everest – will find memories flooding back the moment they step through the front door of the *Pen-y-Gwryd* inn, high above Capel Curig on the A4086 to Llanberis in Snowdonia.

For inside this remote oasis in the mountains is the very bar in which Edmund Hillary and Sherpa Tenzing Norgay, together with all the rest of leader John Hunt's triumphant team, planned in minute detail the climb that was destined to conquer the earth's last untrodden frontier.

Return to that cosy, dark wood-panelled bar today and you can gaze into a display cabinet showing rather more than the average family collectables. In it, for example, are the very length of rope that connected Hillary and Tensing as they stood together on top of the world, the map, woollen hat and string vest of expedition leader Lord Hunt, and the penknife, goggles and umbrella of George Lowe.

What are not on display, however, are the personal memories of Nick Pullee, co-proprietor these days with bother Rupert, and grandson of Chris Briggs, boss man of the Pen-y-Gwryd back in those days of the Everest triumph.

'I wasn't born in 1953, of course, but the whole team came back here for a reunion every year until 1998 and I remember as a small boy being given piggyback rides by Tensing. It wasn't just the planning they did here, apparently. Snowdonia is very similar to the Himalayas on a smaller scale and they used the mountain to practise carrying oxygen cylinders on their backs, using radio equipment and things like that.'

A study of that showcase also explains one of the mysteries which had fascinated me for many years before becoming a journalist – just how did the *Times* achieve a world exclusive for the early editions of its Coronation Day paper?

Climbing with the expedition, at least during its early stages, was *Times* journalist James (later Jan) Morris and revealed inside the cabinet were the code words used in all messages from on high, which only Morris could interpret.

'Postponed,' for example, was either 'Robinson' or 'Knighthood', 'Abandoned' became 'Grasshopper' or 'Washington', 'Injured' equalled 'Acropolis' or 'Olympus' and 'Ill' came out as 'Margarine' or 'Cockfighting'. Significantly, neither 'We've done it!' nor 'Dead' appeared on the list – perhaps for superstitious reasons – but such secrets must have been known to the *Times* man on the spot. (Tensing, incidentally, was either 'Asparagus' or 'Carpenter'; Hillary came out as 'Jerkin' or 'Candlestick' and Hunt was invariably announced as 'Kettle' or 'Stringbag'.)

Chris Briggs, who later handed the business down to his daughter Jane and her husband Brian Pullee, was a hugely influential man of Snowdon, being the founder of the first mountain rescue post, and it was the initial letters of his hotel that accounted for the name given to the most common route to the summit – the internationally famed Pyg Track.

'Most of the people who stay here are walkers or climbers,' says Nick, 'but what we are mostly is a pub. Arrive here around 4pm on a Saturday during the summer and it's hard to get to the bar. Not many people can resist a pint after coming down Snowdon.'

To the uninitiated, the *Bat and Ball* at Hambledon, Hampshire, may not look like the birthplace of a great British countryside tradition that was destined to reach every corner of the British Empire. But this unspectacular red brick pub was where landlord Richard Nyren presided over the newly-formed Hambledon Cricket Club in the late 18th century, which turned an esoteric rustic pastime into a national sport.

Indeed, it was here on Broadhalfpenny Down that Nyren's history-making players, more of a pub side than a village team, thrashed an All-England XI by an innings and 68 runs in 1777 – an achievement recognised by the simple monument that adorns the site today, emblazoned with two curiously shaped bats and a wicket looking more like a croquet ring than the stumps which were to replace it.

Incidentally, 1777 was not only the date of the defining battle of Saratoga Springs in the American War of Independence but things were also going sharply downhill back at home in the life story of the great British Pub.

While its whole survival was threatened by the rowdy binge drinkers of the gin palace era, Samuel Dubleton began his family's half-century tenancy of the antique *Fox and Hounds* in Great Brington, Northamptonshire, that very same year, with a clause in his licence requiring him 'not knowingly to introduce, permit or suffer any bull, bear or badger-baiting, cock fighting or any such amusement in any part of the premises.'

In less gory times, the *Fox and Hounds*, otherwise known as the *Althorp Coaching Inn*, with its stone and wooden floors, black beams and roaring log fires, made further claims upon the annals of history when its glorious beer gardens became part of the playground of the village's favourite daughter, the little girl who would grow up to become the much loved Princess Diana.

Although immensely popular productions of Shakespeare's plays have been performed in its wonderfully ancient and atmospheric courtyard for over half a century, the rightful fame of the *George* in Huntingdon, Cambridgeshire, has nothing to do with the Bard or his followers.

It is no exaggeration to say that there never would have been an English Civil War without the *George's* vital contribution to British history. For it was in this very inn, then owned by his grandfather, that Oliver Cromwell was born in 1599.

Would Charles I have made the *George* his headquarters during the months leading up to his final undoing at the Battle of Naseby in 1645 if he'd known he was dining and sleeping under the very same roof that had sheltered his hated adversary's birthplace?

And did anyone point out the irony at the time?

Almost certainly not.

The licensee of the Great British Pub has always known when it's best to keep his mouth shut.

Chapter fourteen

Playing the game

Many of the sports and games that add spice and thunderous partisanship to everyday lives in the nation's towns and villages would probably just about survive without the backing of the Great British Pub. Soccer, rugby, cricket, tennis, golf and the rest of the biggies would like as not keep their flags flying – even though the advent of the Murdoch Age means that most of their enthusiastic followers would never actually get to watch them being played at national or international level without there being a handy pub in which to see them on Sky TV.

But how many households contain the basic requisites for a quick game of darts, dominoes, pool, bagatelle, bar billiards, shove ha'penny, quoits, ringing the bull, devil among the tailors, skittles – indoors or alfresco – or even cribbage?

THE LEWES ARMS

And were it not for such worthy establishments as the *Lewes Arms*, whose charming maze of little bars lurk beneath the castle ramparts in Lewes, East Sussex, where on earth would you get to enjoy a spot of dwyle flunking?

It could be that there are those dwelling in remoter regions of the United Kingdom, or indeed the rest of the world, who have seldom, if ever, had the opportunity to flunk the occasional dwyle – but that is certainly not the fault of the many pubs in East Anglia and south-east England that resolutely keep a great tradition alive.

Allow, if you will, Rebecca Quinn, assistant manager of the *Lewes Arms*, to brief us all on how to get started.

'First two teams of eight line up for a formal clothing inspection, winning points from the judge for strict adherence to the dress code – straw hat, waistcoat, white baggy trousers or skirt (tied around the knees with garden twine to prevent rats running up legs), and spotted neckerchief.

'Then comes a really important stage – each player must attempt to bribe the judge, with points again awarded according to the pleasure with which each gift is received...'

'And after that, we are ready to start.' Thank you, Rebecca.

OK then, will the fielding team please form a circle – or 'girter' – and start to revolve in time to the music, while the first member of the batting side – the 'flunker' or, in certain areas, the 'driveller' – positions himself in the middle, rotating in the opposite direction? When the music stops all players come to a standstill and, without a moment's hesitation, the flunker must take his stick ('swadger'), with a bar cloth soaked in stale beer wrapped round the end (the 'dwyle'), and hurl his dwyle with the intention of hitting his selected member of the girter on arm or leg (one point), torso (two points) or head (three points.)

If he misses the target altogether – are you following me so far? – he is obliged to down a pint of beer in the time it takes for the girter to complete a single complete rotation.

At this stage it would perhaps be helpful to quote from the official rule book, kept by Rebecca under lock and key in a desk drawer:

> *A flunk is considered finished when the dwyle comes to a halt in one of the following manners:*
>
> > *1. By hitting a member of the opposition forming the girter;*
> >
> > *2. By hitting passers-by, spectators, officials, dogs or other flunkers;*
> >
> > *3. By hitting the ground, wall or fence;*
> >
> > *4. By not leaving the pail of old stale beer even though the flunker has attempted a flunk.*

'It should be added that another way in which a flunk can be finished is by the dwyle hitting a passing car because the game is played on the road outside the pub, which we are not allowed to close to traffic,' Rebecca added helpfully. 'When each of the sixteen flunkers has flunked twice the game is over, with the judge – providing he or she is still sober enough to complete the scoring – announcing the winning team.'

Historians believe that dwyle flunking – or dwile flonking – originated in Suffolk in 1585 but it certainly passed into oblivion for many years until revived in Beccles, Suffolk, in 1966, when an ancient copy of the rules was discovered in an attic in nearby Bungay. Bravo!

Most of us above a certain age were once the proud owners of a mixed variety of glass marbles but what we actually did with them was a matter of personal choice and innovation. There is, however, a set of rules dating back at least to the 16th century and the reign of Elizabeth I – for that is when two ardent gentlemen, one from Sussex and the other from Surrey, competing for the hand of a young maiden of Tinsley Green, near Crawley in West Sussex, and finding themselves still neck and neck after sundry bouts of fencing, wrestling and horse racing settled the matter with a highly charged game of marbles. (Although, who won and whether the good lady accepted the verdict does not appear to be recorded.)

Almost on the same spot where that fateful match took place local teams, with international entrants from all over Europe and sometimes from the United States and Canada, still converge on the *Greyhound Inn* every Good Friday for the British and World Marbles Championship, under the watchful gaze of organisers Sam and Julia McCarthy-Fox.

'We play on Good Friday because, believe it or not, when the modern championships were launched in 1932 marbles was one of the very few games allowed to be played during Lent,' says Julia.

Played on a specially constructed concrete raised ring of six-foot diameter, covered with fine sand, in the middle of the car park, the annual battle royal usually attracts between eighteen and twenty-two teams, is watched by several hundred enthralled spectators and was once covered live by Sky Sports. Serious stuff, indeed.

For those wishing to get started immediately, you need 49 marbles in the middle of the ring and each player chooses his target marble or 'tolly' which, when his turn comes, he aims at the assembled marbles, hoping to remove at least one from the field of play. ('Hence the raised ring,' explains Julia; 'if the marble falls over the edge it is out and if it doesn't it's in – it resolves a lot of disputes.') If this is achieved, his next shot will be from the spot where his tolly comes to rest so a real pro must impose a spin on his shoot, in order to stop his tolly dead in its tracks at the most advantageous position for his next shot. The first team to remove 25 marbles from the ring is declared the winner.

'Some people choose to use a glass tolly and others a ceramic one but the weight doesn't really matter – it's a matter of accuracy,' says Julia. 'Teams are supposed to be here by 10.30 and we hope to get under way an hour later and finish by about 6pm but if it rains the sand gets slushy and tends to slow up the marbles.

'The Dutch and French frequently send a team but Germany never fails. Sometimes they come to drink and sometimes to win – they usually do one or the other but never both.'

The most successful player on each team gets to compete in the individual championship and the walls of the bar are adorned with pictures of the all-time greats such as 'Pop' Maynard, 'Red Pole' Gibbs and 'Captain Marble' himself – Colin Gates.

If you feel like a go at Ringing the Bull, one of the most ancient sporting challenges devised by the Great British Pub, you could do far worse than pop down to that most unspoilt of ancient watering holes, the *Rock* at Chiddingstone, in Kent. And, once there, you would be well advised to persuade Mo Coldman, sister-in-law of licensee Matt Coldman, off her stool at the bar to give a demonstration of how it should be done.

From one wall in the bar protrudes a magnificent bull's head (only here at the Rock it happens to belong to a water buffalo) with a hook on his nose. The ring over the hook is on one end of a string, attached at the other end to the ceiling.

All you have to do is remove the ring from its hook, walk away to wherever in the room takes your fancy, release the ring with a gentle push and send the ring in a trajectory which enables it to reattach itself to the hook on the bull's nose. Easy? Just try it. Or, if you prefer not to make a complete idiot of yourself, don't.

Step forward Mo. Standing a few yards away from the target in the middle of the bar, the first go narrowly missed and the second landed bang on the nose. Taking up a position immediately alongside the bull/buffalo, she then projected the ring out into the room, whereupon it circled straight back on to the ring. You could almost hear the drums rolling as she sat in the chair immediately beneath the target, dispatched the ring into a circular flight and, as the other occupants of the bar held their breath, watched it return unerringly to its mother hook.

'She's obviously spent far too much of her life in the bar,' said her husband, Graham.

The rules are simple enough. Two players attempt to ring the bull. When each succeeds he or she then has ten further throws and the highest number of hits wins the day.

(Approaching his 85th birthday, the pub's oldest regular, Roy 'Uncle' Jenner, was missing from his usual stool on the day I passed by. 'He was 14 when he first came in and he would tell you a tale or two,' said Mo. 'When he first had a vote in a General Election he was on his way to the polling station, popped in to the pub for a pint on his way and that's as far as he got. He admitted the other day that he has never voted in his life because in sixty odd years he has never yet managed to get past the pub.' There's loyalty for you.)

I came across table skittles, or Devil-Among-The-Tailors as it is traditionally known, for the first time in the wonderfully ancient *George* in Castle Cary, Somerset, although it is certain that it was not around for Charles II to have a go when he popped in there for a livener while fleeing from Cromwell's troops after his hiding at the Battle of Worcester in 1651.

If his ghost were to return, however, he would doubtless delight in studying the skills of barmaid Gail, who was happy to take time off to teach me the rudiments of the game. She arranged the nine pins in a diamond formation on the board and then took up the ball (or 'devil') on the end of a chain which was attached to the top of a pole. Pulling the devil towards her and propelling it forwards in a clockwise direction around the pole, she succeeded in demolishing seven of the pins (or 'tailors') in one fell swoop, disposing of the other two in only the second shot of the three she was allowed. (Do not ask how I got on; a chap has his pride. 'It's just a matter of practice,' said Gail modestly.)

Again for the statistically minded, if all tailors disappear in either one or two goes they are repositioned allowing each player a maxim of 27 points. The winning target is usually 101 or 121 but, just as in darts, this score has to be reached exactly – to overshoot sends you back to the status quo. It's great fun, I assure you, and several pints can slip down without being noticed.

Sadly, outdoor skittles has all but disappeared from the British pub scene but other indoor forms are still popular. Hood skittles, as played in Leicestershire and Northamptonshire with slightly different 'cheeses' but similarly strange tables whose protective hood renders a kind of armchair appearance, involves no small investment for any new pub wanting to join the fray.

Paul Moss, landlord of the *Hollybush* in Lutterworth, Leicestershire, where a ladies', men's and mixed team does battle every Monday, Wednesday and Friday in turn, proudly produced his £300 set of three yellow cheeses and led me to his hand-crafted table, or 'board', which recently set him back a cool £1,300. 'It's been worth every penny,' he said – 'the locals love it, and so do our opponents.'

And let no one doubt the importance which the regulars of the *Rose and Crown*, in nearby Thurnby, place on their magnificent full-size skittles ally, revealed by parting the tables and chairs and rolling back the carpet in the pub's function room. On one wall a large notice, bearing the date of April 2, 1927, lays down the law in no uncertain terms:

> *Four members with the President and Treasurer and Secretary shall constitute the Committee and have full power to manage the*

affairs of The Club, also be empowered to settle all disputes that may arise in connection with The Club. The yearly subscription be five shillings payable in advance and no member shall be allowed the use of the alley whose subscription is more than a month in arrear.

When it comes to the serious business, there's no place for short arms and long pockets down at the *Rose and Crown*.

One pub that owns its own permanent double tenpin bowling alley is the wonderfully ancient *Sheep Heid Inn* at Duddingston, Edinburgh, which has been serving pints and drams to its regulars since 1360. And because the alley, opened some 130 years ago and believed to be the oldest in the world, is separate from the pub, it can be hired out for adults' or children's parties for as little as £50 for an entire evening or £12.50 an hour during the day.

Arguably the two most popular pub games are darts and dominoes – and nowhere do they come together more purposefully than in the *Atherton Arms*, in Atherton, Lancashire. For here in the typically friendly environment often associated with the miners' welfare or the working men's club, it has a huge, designated games room that contains not one but four specialist domino tables. And what precisely is a domino table? Well it has an appropriate rectangular shape designed to accommodate a typical final formation, with flanges to prevent tiles flying on to the floor in a moment of excitement and – most important of all – a shelf beneath to house pints of ale so that no accidental spillage is allowed to soil the field of play.

In one corner of the room, the darts board is surrounded by pictures of, and messages from, some of the greats who have come here over the years – such giants of the game as three-times world champion Canadian-born John Part, fellow countryman Gary (The Mauler) Mawson and local hero Matt 'Superman' Clark.

If that endorsement is not enough to establish the pub's sporting credentials, the centre of the room is dominated by a pool table and full-size snooker table.

And if you want a quick chat with the darts champion to end all darts champions, Phil Taylor, he could well be enjoying a quickie at

Cheers Bar, Fraserburgh, Aberdeenshire; and if you ask him nicely he will certainly take you on for a game of pool. They play just about anything at *Cheers*.

But where, I ask you, would we be without the *Crown* at Bedfield in deepest Suffolk? Despite the unremarkable salmon pink exterior of this remote country pub, the lovely landlady, Jackie Grice, claims no fewer than ten games lie on the agenda within. If you allow the weekly quiz night as one, there's bar billiards, darts, shove ha'penny, devil-among-the-tailors, dominoes, boxo (otherwise known as shut-the-box), crib, 'pokey dice' (a sequence of throws which apparently determine whose turn it is to buy the next round – in direct challenge to *Greaves' Rules*) and – wait for it – 'Caves'.

'We think we have the last remaining Caves table in Britain,' said Jackie, leading me to a board attached to one wall containing five cut out circles towards which matching quoits must be aimed. 'To be honest, we're not entirely sure of the rules but each target is worth one to five and you have to score exactly 21 to win.'

Until a year or two ago Jackie used to stage an annual Pub Olympics, with sixteen contestants participating in what can only be described as the Bedfield Octathlon (only the quiz and, I think, the pokey dice were excluded from the menu) and the mighty trophy still stands in the cabinet.

'It's only a very small village and I'm afraid we can't get quite enough entrants to keep it going nowadays,' she said, with heavy resignation. 'To be honest, we're not that well supported by the locals but we don't have a mortgage any more. We have a lot of fun and we're definitely here to stay.'

Neuadd Arms Hotel

But nowhere does the love of sport and the spirit of competition reach a higher – or, some might say, ludicrous – level than at the *Neuadd Arms*, at the heart of Britain's smallest town, Llanwrtyd Wells, in the foothills of the Brecon Beacons in mid-Wales.

It was back in 1980 when then-landlord Gordon Green overheard a heated bar discussion on the subject of whether man could ever beat a horse and rider over a significantly long cross-country course – and immediately announced the world's first Man v Horse challenge.

The bookmaking firm of William Hill joined in the fun by offering a £1,000 prize for the first man to come home first, increasing by a further £1,000 per annum until it was claimed. It took until the twenty-fifth race in 2004 for Huw Lobb (an Englishman, despite the first-name spelling) to pick up a cool £25,000 by completing the gruelling 22-mile course in an astonishing two hours.

'At that stage William Hill pulled out and we couldn't afford to repeat the original deal,' says landlord, Lindsay Ketteringham, who has taken over as chairman of the founder's Green Events organisation. 'So we decided to offer a fixed prize of 1,000 guineas a year – after all it is a horse race of sorts – which is just as well because it was claimed again just three years later.'

Until the late 20th century, pony trekking was the main source of income for the town but this collapsed when government subsidies were withdrawn and everyone in the accommodation and leisure business was threatened with ruin.

That was when the *Neuadd Arms* guv'nor called a crisis meeting, looking for further ideas to bring the visitors flooding in. 'One of the ladies present jokingly said that all she had to offer was 'a bog at the bottom of my garden' but one thing led to another and we decided to stage the World Bog Snorkelling Championship,' recalls Lindsay.

A 30-yards ditch was cut in the adjoining terrain, filled with water and competitors were invited to clad themselves in whatever they thought was appropriate, put on flippers and complete two lengths of the course, without once surfacing. They were allowed to employ a doggie-paddle to assist their progress but no breast stroke or crawl.

'Australia now holds bog snorkelling championships, where they cut a trench in the desert and get the fire brigade to fill it with water. And they're held in the Republic of Ireland, where there is no shortage of bogs, but our next project is to begin a UK bog snorkelling grand prix by inviting Scotland and England to cut suitable trenches,' says the landlord, somehow managing to look deadly serious.

The World Mountain Bike Bog Snorkelling Championships, 'with bikes specially weighted to keep them and their riders beneath the surface,' and the annual Bog Snorkelling Triathlon – no, you don't need to hear the rules – complete the underwater events which are now responsible for bringing tourists to the town from all over the world.

And if that isn't enough, the year's calendar also includes the Real Ale Wobble, when enthusiastic beer cyclists can enjoy a couple of tipple stops along the route and another on the finishing line as a start to the town's ten-day beer festival.

Leaving aside such delicious eccentricity, however, it is that duo of eternal survivors, darts and dominoes, that remain the life blood of the rural British pub – both for the financial benefit of the boozer itself and the wellbeing of the community it serves.

And where better to find the two games in rude good health than the *Fountain*, in Hawes, North Yorkshire, where landlord Angus McCarthy was secretary of the Upper Wensleydale Darts League for 16 years until 2009 and has held the same position with the Upper Wensleydale Dominoes League since the turn of the century?

Not to be left out, his irrepressible wife Mandy leads the pub's ladies' darts team into action every Sunday evening during the winter months.

'From October to Easter there's about thirty weeks when there's not much tourism around and time can hang heavy for the locals, too,' says Angus. 'We've got about 16 different pub teams in the darts league at any one time, and similar for the dominoes, and as well as the weekly league games there are cup matches, knock-out competitions and even one-off Christmas darts and domino knock-outs. One Christmastime recently we had five boards up at the same time, with sixty entries and 150 people in the pub – quite a night!

I have sometimes popped in for a livener at *The Fountain* on my way north to Scotland on assignment or on pleasure and can vouch for the friendly rivalry that sometimes spills into roars of approval and occasional outbursts of applause.

'Rivalry? You can say that again,' confirms Angus. 'Would you believe we actually have player-poaching before the season begins? If anyone plays one game of darts or dominoes for one pub he or she can't switch to another pub during that same season. So there are a few free pints knocking about for the top talents during the run-in to October...'

Daft? Maybe. 'But if our experience is anything to go by,' says Mandy, 'the bad days for the pub trade are beginning to turn the corner.'

So that must be a bull's eye for the Great British Pub if ever there was one. Play up, play up, play the game – and keep the till chiming...

Between rounds...

And talking of sport...

Towards the end of the 1960s when the county cricket championship was still largely an annual competition to determine who would finish second to Yorkshire, I was sent to the wilds of Bradford to interview that most obdurate of win-at-all-costs skippers, the determinedly square-jawed, bald-headed Brian Close.

Just what Brian had done to deserve my attention on this particular occasion I cannot recall and nor is there now any way of finding out because not one word from the encounter made it into next morning's *Daily Mail*.

On my way back to London, however, I found myself overtaken by thirst while passing through Holmfirth, then an undistinguished little township clinging to the foothills of the Pennines, undisturbed by the later fame that came from being the home of Compo, Nora Batty *et al* in *Last of the Summer Wine*.

Pubs, even when sparsely occupied, usually exude an aura of cheery chatter and as soon as I walked in to the *Elephant & Castle* it was obvious that something serious – even, perhaps, terminal – had happened. Long faces huddled in solemn groups, only occasionally punctuating the uneasy stillness with mumbled monosyllables.

A discreet enquiry of the barman soon established the cause of the gloom. The outside wall of the *Elephant & Castle* was home, it transpired, to a fig tree. Not any old fig tree but the most northerly fig tree in Britain. Nay, the only fig tree, apparently, north of the Trent.

In truth, the locals only had the word of 65-year-old professional gardener John Sugden that it was a fig tree at all because until that June of 1968 it had never actually produced a fig.

But that summer it did. A net was erected around it to protect it from wind and bird. A custodian was duly appointed to tender to its every need. The long-awaited fruit had at last taken its bow.

And some time during the night of June 29, 1968, someone had swiped it.

The police had finished their initial enquiries at the scene. Photographs of a barren stalk had been taken from every angle. Even detailed descriptions of the stolen fig had found their way into the police constable's notebook. Rival pub darts team captains or anyone else with a possible motive for the outrage were doubtless already being tracked down.

Any human funeral would long ago have started resonating to the raucous laughter of half-remembered anecdotes, interspersed with beer-fuelled assertions that 'it's what he would have wanted' but somehow such jocularity seemed inappropriate to the passing of a fig.

And next morning, the nicked fig of Holmfirth made an exclusive page lead in all editions and no questions were ever asked on how I had managed to become the only interviewer ever to fail to get anything newsworthy out of dear old Closey. Even more remarkably, the ensuing days brought no claim of a more northerly British fig tree, with or without attachment. I was the hero of the hour.

All of which merely goes to prove that if you are a reporter of world or national events it is never safe to pass a British pub.

Take the time, for example, when I chanced into the *Marquess Tavern* in Islington, north London, and fell into casual conversation with a friendly local postman at the bar.

His daughter, it transpired, had just completed her first morning as an all-purpose assistant at the local branch of a supermarket chain which, just at that time, was conducting a national advertising campaign under the slogan *Good Food Costs Less at Sainsbury's.*

And as her very first task she was despatched to the newspaper and magazine section with the instructions, fresh in from head office, to unclip the staples on all editions of that week's *Radio Times* and remove the centre four pages – which just happened to be an advertising supplement for rivals Tesco – and then reclip the remaining pages into place.

I hastened to buy a copy from her branch and, thus armed, rang the press office of Sainsbury's, which duly denied any such instruction. When I found another store with its *Radio Times* similarly denuded, however, the same spokesman 'discovered' that such a command had gone out from an overenthusiastic young manager but had been quickly rescinded.

Next morning, the front page of the *Daily Telegraph* carried the whole story – under the inspired headline: *Good Magazines Weigh Less at Sainsbury's*.

And then – are you getting the message? – there was the time I decided to kill half an hour or so in a London pub never previously visited, the *King's Head* in Moscow Road, Bayswater.

Here again I was met by a wall of silence, except that somehow this time it had a more comfortable texture about it. Tension there undoubtedly was – but now it was mixed with companionship, team support and no little spellbound fascination.

Again, the reason soon became apparent. This was no ordinary pub. It was, apparently, a chess pub. All over the saloon bar, heads were bowed over kings, queens and humble pawns, time clocks were regularly being clouted and at one table in particular a small crowd had gathered. For here seated was the *King's Head* team which had qualified for next day's finals of the British Chess Championships. A pub team in the nation's most prestigious competition? It had never been heard of. And the team was even enjoying a light-hearted eve-of-Agincourt workout with Raymond Keene, a British grandmaster and chess columnist of the time.

Andrew Whiteley, a pub regular who was to lead the team into battle next day, suddenly looked at his board with momentary puzzlement, discovered he had accidentally knocked off a rook with his pint pot and reached down to the floor to recover it.

'It's one of the best reasons for castling early,' he told me with a grin. 'While the rook is still perched on the corner of the board and you are in a pub it is always susceptible to that kind of a fate.'

The headline in the paper next day was *Pints and pawns down in the snug*.

Indeed, only once do I recall a time when the pub was not the investigative reporter's ideal – if accidental – start point.

Remember how George Davis, jailed for armed robbery in 1975, was subsequently freed after his wife Rose and friends launched a massive '*George Davis is innocent – OK?*' campaign which included the heretical digging up of the Headingley cricket wicket on the eve of an England v Australia ashes test?

When a couple of years later he was caught red-handed, re-arrested and imprisoned after admitting another bank robbery in Seven Sisters Road, his battle-scarred wife was said to be furious with the man who had reneged on all her loyal support.

Now a *Daily Mail* feature writer, perhaps having lost that survival instinct which went with 'sharp end' service both at home and abroad, I chose to begin my background enquiries in the only way I knew how – a visit to the *Blind Beggar* pub, in London East End's Whitechapel Road.

This was not only the pub where William Booth delivered the 1894 sermon that led to the creation of the Salvation Army but was also the venue for Ronnie Kray's murder of a guy called George Cornell, an associate of the equally infamous Richardsons, which came to exemplify the London gangland era of the 1960s. If anyone knew what the score was, this is where I would surely find him.

I bought a pint and, upon delivery, leaned over the counter to confide in the barman that I was from the *Mail* and wondered whether anyone could tell me a bit about George Davis and what the locals were saying about his re-arrest.

Next door to me on the customers' side a chap who turned out to be the landlord took me by the shoulder and led me, not unkindly, to the pavement – leaving my unsipped pint on the counter.

Once outside, I will never forget his words. 'Walk away,' he said. 'Don't run, don't look behind you, just walk. I'll try to watch your back. Maybe no one heard you. With any luck you might just have got away with it.'

I didn't pause to enquire what was on the menu if someone had overheard my question. I didn't run. I walked.

Just for once the best place to start had not been the pub. In the lifetime experience of one devoted seeker of truth and enlightenment it was the solitary exception that surely proves the rule.

Chapter fifteen

Usually reliable sources

The sort of newspaper stories that are far too good to invent nearly always spring from a pub.

So if you don't happen to be in the pub at the time then you don't get to hear the one about the budgerigar and the walrus. Or the Llama that somehow made it home from Cusco to Bishops Stortford. Or, indeed, the barmaid who turned up for work after being molested by a lion.

But if it's true that the Great British Pub is the most productive source of really interesting news stories – as opposed to all those minor wars and political upheavals around the world and economic crises nearer to home which we are all supposed to be interested in – then it's equally true that the most productive of all was not technically speaking a pub at all.

But back in the days when everything that happened north of Aberystwyth was covered from the great Manchester offices of the Fleet Street dailies, just about every news item that had its origins anywhere near the mouth of the River Mersey sprang from the jungle drums of the *Liverpool Press Club*.

Now, the *Press Club* was, in everything except name, a pub. And a brilliant one, to boot. You didn't have to join it – or, at least, I never remember doing so – and the only two differences between it and newspaper pubs everywhere else were the typewriters along one wall and the fact that it remained open all day. In every other respect, the bar, the chatter and the predictable to-ing and fro-ing of its regulars was indistinguishable from every *Red Lion* and *White Swan* elsewhere in the land.

The reason why all news items, however extraordinary, emanated from that one bar (and, no matter how exclusive they were originally deemed to be, would appear in every paper next morning) was the existence of the notorious Liverpool Ring. And the reason why I was privy to its secret code was because Liverpool was the terrain of those two fine *Mail* reporters, Arthur Redford and Clive Freeman, and when either was on day off, the other would do the day shift and I would be despatched from Manchester, booked into the *Adelphi Hotel* and entrusted with the night's coverage.

I quickly learnt the ropes. All bar one of the mighty daily press representatives were not at their 'office' at all – they were either at the *Cavern* or the *Blue Angel* being entertained by the young *Beatles*, *Gerry and the Pacemakers*, Cilla Black or whatever other apostles of the Mersey sound were in town that night.

One man, who had drawn the short straw, stood alone at the bar. If I was luckless enough to be holding the fort and any of the battery of phones rang, invariably it was one of the various Manchester night desks seeking their man. 'Just popped out to buy some fags,' I would say. 'I'll get him to call you.'

An urgent call to either the *Cavern* or the *Blue Angel* would bring not just the sought-after man but the entire corps back to HQ. Whoever was in demand made the required call, received the exclusive tip-off and Phase Two was set in motion. More straws were drawn to decide who should actually go out to cover the newly broken story.

Upon the selected newshound's return, the information would be shared, subtly rephrased here and there, relayed to sundry copytakers and every paper would have the same story, by and large, for next morning's edition.

(Once when a not-to-be-named representative of one of the red tops could not be stirred from his sleep, I stripped my story of all its adjectives, even truncating the occasional verb, and delivered it to an unsuspecting copytaker at his newspaper. It appeared word-for-word next morning – one of my proudest journalistic moments.)

As any reporter who has ever staffed a district office will know, the bollocking that followed a missed story was both more predictable and more eloquent than the herogram that might just occasionally result from an exclusive. It was far better to be safe than sorry.

And anyway, the Mersey sound was just beginning to sweep the world and it was a pity not to be out there, foot-tapping to its pulsating rhythms at first hand. Those were heady days in Lancashire's second city.

Elsewhere it was the more conventional pubs that acted out their role as the street corner information and ideas centres which both assuaged the thirst and filled the notebooks (or at least the memory banks if they were still in working order next morning) of Britain's weekly, evening and morning newspaper reporters.

A year before I was born a guy called Thomas McEntee opened a pub alongside the offices of the *Scottish Daily Express* in Glasgow. Unknown to the outside world, it was actually a part of the Express building accessible from within and it's real name was, and is, *The Press Bar*. But has always been known to its regulars as *Tom's*.

Despatched to have my 'fortune' told by one of those psychiatric agencies that asked quick-fire questions, analysed the answers and told you what sort of a chap you were and what sort of job you might think about doing – in the days when you actually had a choice – I nobly subjected myself to the ordeal on behalf of the *Daily Mail* features editor and arranged for two other guinea pigs to be subjected to the same indignity, the then Provost of Glasgow and the legendary Celtic football club manager, Jock Stein.

(I can't remember how the other two got on, but my summarised outcome was that I tended towards the arrogant, self-centred, irreverent and irresponsible, while being innately fascinated by unimportant trivia and appeared only suited to a career in newspapers. Outraged, I reported the outcome to my wife over the phone and her only response was 'Yes – but how did it *know*?)

Another young lady taking the test was doing so on behalf of the *Glasgow Evening Times* – slightly worrying as the *Mail* invariably sat on such undated features for several days, and she was obviously going to let all rival papers into the idea of doing the same.

Back in *Tom's*, I encountered Charlie Wilson, latterly my deputy news editor in Fleet Street and yet to become a distinguished editor of *The Times* in London, who was currently the young lady's boss man. 'Don't worry, Bill,' he said over the umpteenth chaser, 'you let me know when the *Mail* is running your piece and I'll hold her masterpiece until the afternoon before.' There's friendship for you. But then that's what newspaper pubs were for.

Ironically, back in those far flung days, the *Mail* was the only Fleet Street paper to have its Scottish office in Edinburgh while everyone else was based in Glasgow in general and *Tom's* in particular. What a hell hole. I vividly remember going in but can't ever quite remember leaving.

Another man who admits to occasional bouts of identical amnesia is my old *Daily Mirror* chum, Colin Dunne.

In the absence of a shorthand note, I rely on memory but Colin has an unforgettable turn of phrase. It went something like this:

'At the *Journal* and *Evening Chronicle* in Newcastle the pub, the *Printer's Pie*, was actually within the building and Gordon Chester, one of their top reporting chaps, decided to save himself a lot of travelling and married the barmaid.

'In Manchester, the *Swan with two Necks* in Withy Grove was a jolly hack's boozer until Mike Gagie, newsdesk man, decided to get the champagne cocktails rolling. No one was allowed to refuse. One afternoon it ended up with the entire staff in the pub and the news editor's pleas for them to return raised only hoots of derision.

'Eventually Gagie led the whole crew back in a conga line, singing *Lily the Pink*. They danced into the office of the editor, Mike Terry, and insisted he took a sip of the cocktail. Mike was on no-booze pills at the time and turned a weird shade of dark blue.

'In *McGlade's* bar in Belfast, the IRA stormed in one night, produced guns and demanded money. It was such a wild drunken place, full of reporters, that no one noticed. They had to put bullets in the ceiling to get any attention. The *Europa* in Belfast was blown up so often that when checking in hacks used to request a room with a window.'

Oh stop it, Colin – I believe every word.

(Nowadays, Gordon looks back on those Newcastle days in wonderment that he is still alive. 'I remember the *Printer's Pie* well, of course, but we also drank in the *Lord Chancellor*, the *Black Boy*, the *White Hart* – before they pulled it down to build the new *Chronicle* offices – which I seem to recall was why they had to build the *Printer's Pie* into the new offices – the *Brass Man*, the *Post Office Buffet*, the *Imperial*, the *Farmer's Club* (to fill the gap between afternoon closing and evening opening,) the *County*, the *Victoria and Comet* – always known as the *Spit and Vomit* – the *Forth*, the *Long Bar* – heavens, those were the days!')

Did the paper ever come out, Gordon? Silly question – Geordie newsmen were built of sturdy stuff.

My own recollection of Manchester pubs were the two just around the corner from the *Mail* and *Manchester Evening News* in Hardman Street, the *Victoria* and the *New Theatre* – both now sadly gone, I believe, to make room for the new law courts.

The *New Theatre*, run by the legendary Arthur Gosling with the city's finest range of cheeses alongside some of its best beer, was also home to the *Granada TV* faithful and regular bar-hanger Michael Parkinson famously instructed his reception desk not to say he was in the *New Theatre* but that he had nipped into 'Studio 3'. A quick call to Arthur had him back in no time. Not surprisingly, even Arthur began to believe his pub was called *Studio Three*.

Arthur's father before him used to have the *Sawyer's Arms* in Deansgate, where Sir John Barbirolli was wont to retreat after the rigours of conducting the Hallé Orchestra at the Free Trade Hall. Occasionally entrusted by the *Evening News* to review one of his concerts, I would track Sir John to his hideaway and seek his own verdict. 'The *Schubert* was crap but we got ourselves together for the *Saint-Saens*,' would be a not untypical judgement. My reputation as a music critic quickly soared.

Another Manchester pub much in demand during the wee hours of the night shift was the *Sir John Abercrombie* in Bootle Street. A pre-arranged coded tap on the window alongside the front door would magically cause it to open. Once inside you were quickly among friends, most of them officers from the nearby Manchester police headquarters – so it was always wise to take a notebook with you.

And now – you've been very patient – to the barmaid and the lion. It was that famous *Yorkshire Post* editor, Sir Linton Andrews, who delighted in telling the cautionary tale of the reporter who failed in his duty – by not going to the pub.

It happened when he was previously editor of the *Leeds Mercury* and awoke one morning to discover that his paper was alone among all its rivals in missing the story of a local barmaid who had been bitten by a lion at a music hall in the city. It didn't take long to find out why.

Just like every other night, nearly every late duty reporter had been supping in *Whitelock's Turks Head*, the city's oldest pub and still the regular habitat of Leeds journalists, the previous evening when the luckless lass clocked on, heavily bandaged, to tell the story of her ordeal.

Alone among the absentees was Francis Boyd, later to enjoy a distinguished career as political correspondent of the *Manchester Guardian*, who excused himself on the grounds that he was a Congregationalist and teetotaller. He escaped Andrews' wrath on religious grounds but never forgot the big one that got away.

If Daniel Defoe had met Alexander Selkirk at the *Llandoger Trow* pub in Bristol a few years later than he did, it's a pound to a penny he would never have been able to keep the story of *Robinson Crusoe* to himself.

For the *Llandoger* was destined to become the daily meeting place of that veteran band of West Country men, Chris White of the *Mail*, Sid Young of the *Mirror*, Phil Dampier of the *Sun*, Dave Newman of the *Star* and photographers Johnny Walters (*Mail*) and George Phillips (*Mirror*).

The day when Chris's wife-to-be, Anne, met the gang for the first time, Newman was wearing a trendy jerkin as a body warmer. When Newman complained that no one had told him some detail in a story they had all done that morning, Young said rather unsympathetically that he was in the habit of looking at cuttings and advised Newman to do the same. Newman retorted that the only cuttings Young ever got to see were grass cuttings (Young had a large house with enormous garden – bought with the proceeds of his days as the *Mirror* man in New York). When Sid snapped back 'At least I can afford a jacket with sleeves,' Anne decided it was time to leave,' Chris recalls. 'She generously put it all down to the drink.'

(But Chris is the first to admit that he was well able to hold his corner when it came to downing the pints. When he finally married Anne his new father-in-law was amazed by the massive pile of telegrams to be read out. They turned out to be mostly from pub landlords throughout Avon, Somerset, Devon and Cornwall. And he recalls that they all finished with the same four words: 'We will miss him.' Good on you, Chris.)

Before workaday boozing was largely outlawed around the scattered newspaper offices of London, all the legendary pubs were understandably collected around Fleet Street.

The *Mucky Duck* we have already discussed but many of the others had names that bore no resemblance to anything that appeared on the sign without. The miniscule *Auntie's* disappeared soon after I hit the street in the late sixties and even my old buddy John Edwards can't remember its real name. 'It was the *Mail* pub in its day where Donald Todhunter did much of his hiring and firing,' he recalls. 'And it was pulled down to make a car park – for four cars!' (It was the *Rose and Crown*, John. Our old colleague, Keith McDowell, that most robust of industrial correspondents, not only dutifully bowed to Todhunter's command but his memory seems to have survived longer than ours.)

Neither *Winnie's* nor *Number Ten*, on the right, just up Fetter Lane, was the real name of one of Hugh Cudlipp's favourite boozers either – but what on earth was it called? The *Two Brewers*? Maybe.

And, of course, the pub that ultimately became the *Mirror* staff's number one second home, the *White Hart*, was known as nothing else but the *Stab in the Back*. Only the *King and Keys* (Telegraph) and *Popinjay* (Express), as far as I recall, managed to hang on to their given names.

Veteran *Mirror* man Revel Barker recalls the day he walked into the *Cheshire Cheese* – more often populated by tourists looking for journalists than by journalists themselves – in its little alley just off Fleet Street with *Sunday Mirror* northern news editor, Ken Bennett, only to be told that its lunch tables were fully booked.

The conversation, as he recalls, went something like this:

Barker: Full? Full of what, exactly?

Head waiter: Tourists.

RB: And they are here because...?

HW: Because it's the most historic pub in Fleet Street.

RB: So they come in here expecting to see... what, or whom...?

HW: Oh... OK, I take the point...

And he led them to the corner banquette where he addressed an American family:

HW: Excuse me, sir, but you'll have noticed, when you sat down, that there's a plaque on the wall behind you saying *Dr Johnson. His seat.*

Yank: Oh, sorry... Has he come in?

HW: No, sir. Sadly he died. But before he died he bequeathed his seat to Mr Barker. And now HE has come in...

Yank: Then is it OK if we all shuffle up and make room?

HW (aside): There you go. Now you'd better entertain the buggers.

KB (as we sat down): Did I tell you what Princess Anne said to me last week, the little minx...?

Magic.

And talking of conversational exchanges, how's this for size?

Peter Jackson, that most eloquent of rugby writers, recalls taking his wife, Anne, for the first time into one of Cardiff's two journalistic hideaways, *Roberts Bar*. (The other one was the *Queen's Vaults*.)

'Before she could even sit down,' recalls Jackson, later to become rugby union correspondent for the *Daily Mail* but at the time recently arrived on to the staff of the *South Wales Echo*, 'a reporter on our sister daily, the *Western Mail*, came over and said 'take her out – this is a men only bar.'

'It was my wife's first meeting with John Humphreys...'

Between rounds...

Nowadays the British pub tends to be pretty static on high street or village crossroads but not so long ago it was quite capable of venturing further afield.

It was one evening in February, 1980, that a *Daily Mail* colleague invited me to spend an hour or two with him in his favourite watering hole to wind down at the end of another pressurised day in the office.

The scene, as I recall, was pretty familiar. Mr and Mrs Bob Wright were sitting with Wellington the spaniel in faithful attendance in their usual alcove, where once they did their courting.

David Betts was supping a pint of Ruddles bitter from his personalised pot and about to deal the first hand in the nightly bridge school that he had joined five years earlier.

There was the usual sprinkling of end-of-day shop talk with Stella Hodaszy, an 18-year-old secretary, sipping a well-earned gin and tonic as she went through her notebook with her boss, and three company directors were holding their twice-weekly board meeting over a sundowner or two.

Leaning on a corner of the bar, a couple of cigar-smokers were holding a post-mortem on the success of the regulars' belated Christmas party which had graced this very space the previous night.

But this was not the *Rose and Crown* and neither was it the *Corblimey Conservative Club*.

This was the buffet car of the 6.45pm from Charing Cross to Hastings and the spaniel was looking as self-important as any dog would with its own £299 annual season ticket with 'Mr Wellington' inscribed on the back.

The message was clear. You didn't just catch the 6.45 – you belonged to it. This truly was a pub on wheels.

'There is a chap who has been travelling on this train for two years and he is still only first reserve for the bridge school,' I was told by one of the regulars – 'I'm afraid we're having to keep membership pretty tight.'

'What you have to remember,' explained Bob Wright, displaying Wellington's ticket to my incredulous gaze, 'is that this is just about our entire social life. Nearly all our friends belong to this train and by the time we get home to Battle (in Sussex) it is really too late to go out meeting people.'

On the bridge table the drinks were already assembled. 'We never play for money,' said David, a film production accountant, 'because that's the quickest way to lose friends.' But how, in the absence of a genial landlord, did the quartet manage to keep the same table available for combat for five years?

'We take it in turns to leave the office early and catch the incoming train at Waterloo East and bag our table before the train even arrives in Charing Cross,' he explained. Silly question.

Farther up the bar, Mike Blease, managing director of an international marketing company, had invited Keith Pepin, a Lockheed executive from California, to join him for a meeting.

'I think British Rail would be amazed to discover just how much valuable foreign business is brought into the country by this one pub – sorry, compartment – but we have our fun as well,' said Mike. 'It really is like an exclusive club.'

But a cloud hung over the nightly assembly. So amazed was British Rail to discover that here was a fraternity of passengers that was actually enjoying itself that plans were already afoot to abandon not only this but all its pubs-on-wheels throughout the national network in favour of the stark service counters that exist today.

'You know, I will never understand you British,' said the man from Lockheed. 'The commuter airline I use back home between San Diego and Los Angeles has just removed some of its plane seats – because there wasn't enough room at the bar.'

Maybe the yanks still have a suggestion or two to offer as the Great British Pub fights for survival.

(PS – and what a PS...)

My old pal, John Dodd, *Sun* superstar and born in a pub (see Chapter 18) recalls a similar train for regulars only that used to ply between Portsmouth and London Waterloo.

For 20 years he remembers that daily commute. 'Some of my best friends I met over BR coffees or cans of beer at 80mph and there are still bonds of joint sufferings from the vicissitudes of strikes, line failures, demonic stewards, heatless carriages and diversions through Aldershot that survive the years,' he recalls.

'At various stations up the line people from the newspaper, PR, photographic and advertising worlds, always the latest of starters, would get on and join us, picking up the conversation from the day before, exchanging office gossip.

'There'd be John Hill, the newspaper designer, getting on at Godalming, Terry Fincher, the photographer, Jack Wood the sports writer, Peter Hill, *The Times* business correspondent, Alan Waldie, advertising mastermind of the Benson and Hedges gold pack, all surfacing at Guildford, and then a profusion of other souls jostling aboard at Woking.

'In those days there were two buffet car attendants and a chef, usually survivors of that even then bygone era of great liners or RN wardrooms, who cooked a fairly full range of grills, from the full house of egg, bacon, sausage, tomato and toast to small steaks with an egg on top, down to boiled eggs.

'Going home, free from the turmoil of the day, it was less civilised, the 18.50 and 19.50 buffets straining under queues that frequently stretched into the next carriage while the regulars somehow commandeered their usual tables or outflanked the rest by huddling around the buffet door and ordering drinks from the stewards in a mystical variety of signals.'

But here comes the memory to end all memories, even though John admits he was never a member of the notorious 'W' club that used to ride the range on those Portsmouth-bound evening buffet bar homegoings.

'You became a member by drinking a miniature scotch or whatever every time you passed a station beginning with W, recalls the irrepressible Dodd. 'Since the train started at Waterloo, you were immediately one to the good, and of course that would be followed by Wimbledon, West Byfleet, Weybridge, Woking, Worplesdon, Witley, and, since by then it didn't matter, by Waslemere and Wetersfield as well.'

Doddy, I believe every word of it.

Chapter sixteen

Since records began

Of the British pubs and inns that have survived into the 21st century, claimants to be the oldest, the smallest, the highest, the remotest and all the other superlatives abound in good-natured competition.

The highest (the *Tan Hill Inn* in the Yorkshire Dales) and the remotest (*The Old Forge*, 18 miles from the nearest spot reachable by car on the mountainous west coast of Scotland) have already been unveiled in earlier pages and enjoy unrivalled recognition – after all, who can argue with the boffins of the Ordnance Survey – but to cast judgment on the rival arguments of just about every other category is to open a right royal can of worms.

According to the *Guinness Book of Records*, the oldest pub in England is *Ye Olde Fighting Cocks* in St Albans, Hertfordshire, which actually began life as a giant pigeon house rather nearer to the Abbey than it is today.

'The original building was destroyed at the end of the 16th century and replaced by this one but there has been a pub on this site since 1150, which definitely makes us the oldest in the country,' says landlord Tim Brown. 'And we might be small as pubs go but it must have been a mighty big dove cote in its former life...'

Originally called *The Round House*, it was renamed because of the popularity of its regular cock fights, held in the bar from the early 1800s.

Some original features remain including the main fireplace with bread oven and oak roof beams. There are even tunnels reputedly running from the beer cellar to St Albans Cathedral, previously used by monks on a regular basis.

But John Jewitt, licensee of the *Man and Scythe* in Bolton, Lancashire, does not take the *Guinness* verdict lying down. 'A very early map of Bolton, made in 1490, clearly shows this pub so we know beyond doubt that it existed then,' he says. 'But in documents dated 1253, when the then Earl of Derby was given the rights to the market, there was mention of the church and a pub alongside the market and as there was still only the one pub in 1490 it must have been the same one. The cellar here was built with a technique that has never been used since the year 1200 and there is evidence that a pub was already on this site by the time the parish church was completed in the 11th century. However old the original dove cote which is now The *Fighting Cocks* might be, it certainly hasn't been a pub standing where it is now since long after that.'

Despite its breathtaking antiquity, Jewitt insists it is today a real pub for its 21st-century regulars. 'We don't have TV and the menu is strictly DIY,' he insists. A DIY menu? 'We don't serve any food at all but we invite the locals to bring their own,' laughed the irrepressible host.

Accepting for the time being the generally held view that the date of 1189 boldly displayed on the wall of Nottingham's *Trip to Jerusalem* is dubious to say the least, a fair case could be made for the previously-mentioned *Church House Inn* in Rafferty, Devon, because the building by definition predated the church next door – it would have been a hostel for the workmen recruited to build it – and the first vicar, Geoffrey Hurning, took over his flock in 1199. 'It would certainly have been a brewhouse, where ale would have been brewed and drunk, so it could be said to have been a pub for a few years before that,' says licensee Ray Hardy.

And it is almost indisputable that today's magnificent *Talbot*, in Oundle, Northamptonshire, is the oldest site in continuous use as a pub or inn. Originally known as *The Tabret* – a form of tabard worn by heralds – it was first opened in 638AD by a group of monks as a hostel, providing food, drink and shelter to pilgrims and other travellers and subsequently completely rebuilt as the *Talbot* nearly a thousand years later from stones, windows and beams taken from the ruins of Fotheringhay Castle. And it stayed on exactly the same spot.

But mention any of these worthy claimants in any of the warren of cosy bars that make up the magnificent *Royal Standard of England*, in the village of Forty Green, near Beaconsfield in the heart of the rolling Chiltern Hills, and expect a frosty reception.

Modestly describing itself as the oldest *free house* in England – although it is hard to imagine what other sort of house existed several centuries before the first commercial brewery or pub chain was thought of – the Royal Standard's official history begins with the alehouse that occupied the site for some 500 years *before* it survived the last of Viking raids along the Thames Valley in 1009 and 1010...

After yet another invasion, this time William the Conqueror's 1066 visitation, the alehouse became named *Se Scip* (The Ship) by the local West Saxons and it was not until 1663 that Charles II presented it with its current name in recognition of its landlord's loyalty in giving shelter and support to his executed father and fellow Cavaliers after defeat at the Battle of Worcester. (Although by this time the pub had become a fully-fledged inn with several bedrooms for travellers and the more cynical among its regulars privately ascribed the king's gratitude to the undisputable fact that the landlord turned a blind eye to the upstairs presence from time to time of several of his many mistresses.)

It is by no means certain, however, that the alehouse that occupied the site prior to 1099 was the same building as the present-day *Royal Standard* and another leading contender for the overall title of oldest surviving *British* pub is therefore the *Skirrid Mountain Inn* in the village of Llanfihangel Crucorney, near Abergavenny in the Welsh Brecon Mountains, because today's pub is the very same hostelry that appears in chronicles dated 1110. In its long and often violent 900-years history, it is believed to be where Welsh nationalist hero Owain Glyndwr (anglicised by William Shakespeare as Owen Glendower) rallied his troops for his assault on English sympathisers at nearby Pontrilas in the early 15th century and halfway up the magnificent square spiral staircase is a storeroom once used as the cell in which many a prisoner spent his last night before receiving his death sentence from the ruthless Judge Jefferies in the courthouse below.

And if the *Skirrid Mountain Inn* is unchallenged as the oldest inn in Wales, there can similarly be little doubt that the *Sheep Heid Inn*, in Duddingston, Edinburgh – already featuring elsewhere as being the home of the world's oldest working skittle alley – boasts the same distinction north of the border.

Opening its doors for the first time in 1360, it gained its present name 220 years later when King James VI presented the landlord with a ram's head, a replica of which still hangs on the wall in the main bar area – the original being preserved at nearby Dalmeny House, home of the Earl and Countess of Rosebery, which is open to the public during the summer months.

Again if the *Guinness Book of Records* is to be taken at face value, the smallest pub in Britain is without doubt the diminutive *Nutshell*, in the heart of Bury St Edmunds in Suffolk. Measuring just 15ft by 7ft, the four or five regulars sipping their pints at one end of the bar when I walked in made the place seem packed to the rafters.

But just like the Pekinese that thinks it is a Great Dane, the manager gazed around his empire and denied any such hasty judgment. 'We have live music nights here from time to time,' he declared proudly. 'The band huddles at that end and the customers at the other.'

In truth, although the whole place looks both inviting and perfectly proportioned, the bar area is so small that it is hard to imagine why anyone should have thought of building it as recently as 1867. 'It was built on a piece of land belonging to the pawn brokers' shop next door,' said my informant, to the obvious amazement of the regulars listening in. 'He realised that nearly all his customers pawned their possessions in order to raise enough money to have a drink so he decided to build a pub for them next door so he could get the money back straight away!'

But believe it or not, the *Nutshell* is not without its challengers. Even more remarkably, in a period sadly dominated by pub closures, the latest pretender to the Lilliput throne opened for business only in 2006. Yet the *Signal Box Inn*, in the Lincolnshire seaside resort of Cleethorpes, claims to be not only the smallest pub in Britain but also in the whole world.

And measuring just 64 square feet (compared with the Nutshell's massive 105 square feet), licensee Alan Cowood seems to have statistics on his side.

As its name suggests, the recently opened pub, situated within the Lakeside station on the narrow gauge Cleethorpes Coast Light Railway really is a Victorian signal box, imported from the railway line serving the now-closed Santon iron ore mines at Scunthorpe.

'We couldn't resist it but didn't really know what to do with it,' admits Cowood, himself a working member of the Light Railway company. 'It seemed the most appropriate use was as a garden shed but then someone came along and suggested we turn it into a pub. Fortunately one of our members had a licence so he ran it until I could obtain a licence of my own.'

And exactly how many customers could it comfortably accommodate? 'Two at the bar and four sitting,' said the guv'nor, without the semblance of a smile.

Yet astonishingly, on a busy weekend Alan still manages to empty ten 9-gallon barrels of real ale. 'We have tables and chairs in the beer garden and in the evenings there are railway carriages in which to shelter,' explains the landlord.

Doubtless the *Nutshell* supporters, denied any such outdoor overspill, will argue whether gardens and other outdoor space should count when calculating overall size. I pass.

Between rounds...

Is it beer or is it ale? Or does it matter? Let's be pedantic. The main difference between the beer which is the staple diet of the present-day British pub and the ale which greeted the Roman invaders is that beer uses hops to give it its characteristic bitter flavour – and ale does not. Or, at least, did not – until modern day English usage become a bit blurred on the subject.

Just like 'uninterested' and 'disinterested' and 'relatives and relations', nowadays 'beer' and 'ale' have tended to become interchangeable and, anyway, their history goes back so far that who's counting?

There is no doubt, however, that some sort of ale was brewed by the ancient Egyptians. Although it was already made from barley, wheat, water and yeast – but no hops – it is equally certain that its appearance would not have found favour with today's discerning drinker.

It was often cloudy and the head was so thick that it could not be drunk at all from the surface. As a result it was supped through a hollow reed, similar to the modern drinking straw, often by several people gathered round a single container... the birth of social drinking?

My old pal and *Daily Mail* colleague Vincent Mulchrone, has waxed eloquently – as he has on so many other subjects – on its origins and has come up with the challenging theory that the only reason for its invention in the first place was as a water-purifier. And it is entirely for that reason alone, he asserts, that there are tombs dating back to 6000BC which record the brewing of barley and water, fermented by bread. 'Similar tablets from Mesopotamia,' wrote the great man, warming to his theme, 'show two thirsty-looking characters stirring away at a brewery vat. And Babylon we know had the world's first barmaids. They gave good measure too. The penalty for a short pull was death by drowning.' Vincent's sources were always fiercely protected but we must take his findings with all due respect.

Indeed, the noble wallop is known to have reached Britain by the Neolithic period, providing refreshment for those engaged in the back-breaking business of constructing Stonehenge – gracious me, was ever a pint down the road better deserved? Back in those early days, however, it would have been brewed communally in a village rather than offered for sale and it would have to have been taken 'at the desk' because there would definitely not have been any buildings devoted to its enjoyment.

And even after the Romans arrived with their *tabernae* and the Brits responded by turning their 'taverns' into alehouses, beer went on being brewed in the home, on farms, in wayside drinking-houses and, later, in the monasteries – but there were still no breweries. (In fact, until refrigeration was developed towards the end of the 19th century, beer could be brewed in Britain only during the colder months of the year.)

Though the Norman invaders brought wine across the Channel with them it never caught on with the natives and by 1188 beer was so well established that Henry II imposed a tax on its sale – known to its sufferers as the 'Saladin Tithe' – to help pay for the Crusades. (Needless to say, when the last of the Crusades had been assigned to history, no monarch thought fit to discontinue the tax – and we've been stuck with it ever since.)

After being brewed for the odd millennium as ale without hops, beer finally came to Britain in the 1400s from the Low Countries, where hops were used for both flavour and as preservative, but it took another century and a half before they became accepted as an essential ingredient.

And here, for the sake of the not-many-people-know-that (or WOW!) factor, I can do no fairer than quote from the Brewers & Licensed Retailers Association's excellent little booklet *The Story of Beer* – from which I've nicked a fair amount of info thus far and will shamelessly continue to do so hereafter.

'By the early 1700s, alehouses and taverns would commonly mix two or three beers when serving a pint, with old, dark, well-vatted beers being mixed with fresher, lighter ale. To try and produce one beer which alone matched the taste of such mixtures, brewers in London developed a black, hoppy beer called *entire*. It was instantly popular with the porters working in the markets of Billingsgate and Smithfield and became better known as *porter* after its principal customers.

'In the 1750s, the Irish took porter one stage further and produced a rich, creamy version known as *stout porter*. So successful was this that it rapidly developed as a distinct beer of its own, called simply *stout*.'

How many mellifluous Irish enthusiasts of their treasured Liffy water know that it owes its origins to the proverbially foul-mouthed denizens of London's Billingsgate and Smithfield markets?

Distinctive regional beers have always depended on the quality of the water – or liquor as it is always known in the breweries – and it was the particular combination of minerals in the local water that created the great beer producing centres such as Burton-on-Trent. (Indeed, most brewers now treat their water, whether it comes from mains or wells, with a treatment known as Burtonisation to give it characteristics akin to those that occur naturally at that Staffordshire holy of holies.

But it was not until the early 19th century that Britain's most famous beer emerged when the brewers of Burton sought a new international market for their exclusive 'pale ale' in India, where so many British troops, civil servants, diplomats and soldiers of fortune had taken up residence. In order to survive a long sea journey and a tropical climate, a variant formula had to be produced.

India Pale Ale – of IPA as it is known today – was an instant chart topper. Lighter, clearer and hoppier and therefore more bitter – than most of the beers of its time, its reputation at home was such that it was soon challenging porter for dominance of the market. When the brewery chief was satisfied with the end product of his mix he would announce it to be 'running bitter' – a phrase which prompted the pub customer to demand a 'pint of bitter.'

Bitter actually comes quite late into the modern story of beer, well behind such other favourites as mild, brown and winter ale and the ultra-strong barley wine.

Again it was not until the advent of refrigeration at the end of the 19th century that the brewing of lager, just beginning to creep in from Germany and Czechoslovakia, became possible in Britain – at roughly the same time that Burton brewers were producing the first draught bitter. By the beginning of the 21st century, lager – lighter, colder and less hoppy than the traditional home grown real ales – accounted for approximately half of the beer sales in Britain and 90 per cent of production world wide.

Apart from water, the main ingredient of British beer is barley. Grown on upwards of four million acres of southern England, East Anglia, the Midlands and Scotland, at least 650,000 tonnes of the cereal are required by British brewers annually. The barley is transferred into malt by steeping the grains in water and allowing them to germinate. And it is malt which gives beer its body, its potential strength and much of its flavour.

Hops are grown in south-east England and Hereford and Worcester and traditional British beer uses about a third more hops than lager-type beers. Yeast, a natural and self-duplicating micro-organism, completes the process and is essential to the fermentation which produces alcohol.

By the end of the second millennium and after 2,000 years of the Great British pub, more than 1,200 different beers were being brewed in the UK and somewhere around 29 million pints consumed every day.

Cheers!

Chapter seventeen

Yo ho ho…

Over the two thousand years' history of the British Pub there have been social and economic watersheds that have brought near disaster and others that have unexpectedly brought a new wave of customers – but probably the arrival of William of Orange and Mary on to the throne remains the only epoch that somehow managed to do both at the same time.

For not only did William III's determination to stamp out French imports of wine and brandy and his championship of a good British-made alternative spawn the notoriously riotous 'gin palaces' that sprang up throughout the nation, particularly in the city and town centres between 1720 and 1750, creating a mighty and influential force of temperance campaigners to threaten the very survival of the British pub, it also launched a new and lawless trade in smuggled spirits from the continent and the Caribbean.

And the smugglers, seeking safe houses from which to launch their fearsome raids and in which to store their ill-gotten gains, quickly brought unexpected custom and wealth to the pubs of Cornwall, Devon and along the edge of the English Channel as far as Sussex and Kent.

Just look what they did for *Jamaica Inn*, tucked away alongside the A30 at Bolventor on the windswept Bodmin Moor. 'As pubs go, this is probably the most famous in the country,' says general manager Steven Carr, not a man to mince his words. And gazing around at the complex tourist attraction it has become, who can doubt his claim?

Although built in 1750 and almost immediately a pivotal player in the great age of the smuggler – at the time it was estimated that half the brandy and a quarter of the tea arriving in Britain as contraband was landed along the Devon and Cornish coast and the quantity of incoming rum probably accounted for its name – Carr would be the first to admit that its magnetic appeal to visitors to the West Country is probably ascribable more to Daphne du Maurier's epic tale of the same name than to the lawless anti-heroes of its early history.

But step inside, especially when an almost routine gale is whistling across the moor, and the warmth of the welcome and the profusion of smuggling and du Maurier family artefacts quickly evoke a colourful past – by no means diminished by the plaque on the floor bearing the words 'On this spot Joss Merlyn was murdered.'

(Modern travellers, unfamiliar with du Maurier's novel, should be reassured that homicide is not a regular occurrence among these friendly beer pumps. The dreadful Merlyn was, of course, the evil 7ft tall bully, given to fearsome bouts of boozing, who, when queried by his heroine niece, Mary Yellan, why he chose to run a business which appeared to have no paying customers, replied 'I'm not drunk enough to tell you why I live in this god-forsaken spot and why I'm the landlord of Jamaica Inn.' So fear not – the ill-fated Joss Merlyn never existed except in the fertile imagination of a truly gifted storyteller.)

Although separated now from the sea by many miles of tortuous roads, two centuries ago Bolventor lay at the heart of a web of pack animal tracks which criss-crossed Bodmin Moor and were known only to the locals who traversed them. And by such tracks, the securely isolated *Jamaica Inn* stood little more than a dozen miles from Looe and Polperro to the south and Trebarwith, Tintagel and Boscastle to the north – the ideal hoarding place for the valuable but dangerous cargo *en route* for Devon and beyond.

'We're still a genuine pub with a full range of beers and a few farming regulars,' insists Carr, 'but, yes, thanks to Daphne du

Maurier, we're mostly in the holiday trade and our 16 letting rooms are full most of the time.'

Smugglers don't come with any more ferocious reputation than Coppinger, that giant Dane who terrorised the Devon and Cornwall coasts towards the end of the 18th century and who allegedly discouraged the attentions of excise men by arranging to have one of them beheaded.

The labyrinth of bars and beams and friendly welcome that await today's visitors to *Hoops inn* at Horns Cross, just a mile away from the sea on the A39 in North Devon, makes it hard to believe that this was once Coppinger's local, where he and his gang probably planned many of their darkest deeds.

Behind its romantic thatched exterior, *the Cat and Fiddle* near the Hampshire village of Hinton Admiral nowadays has a fairly bland modernised interior, but stand in front of the fireplace, close your eyes and it is easy enough to picture a scene of far more exciting skulduggery.

For behind this very ingle was once the secret hiding place for smuggled brandy and behind it a subterranean passageway running deep into the protective foliage of the New Forest.

(Customers not caring to ponder such lawless times, however, may care to smile at the rather lighter quotation in the bar, ascribed to the peerless W C Fields: A WOMAN DROVE ME TO DRINK AND I NEVER EVEN HAD THE COURTESY TO THANK HER.)

Similarly, travel further east along the coast and today's patrons of the historic *Royal Oak*, in Langstone, are more likely to be gazing over the rim of their foaming pints towards Hayling Island and at low tide feasting their eyes on a magnificent turnout of wading birds playing on the acres of mud lying exposed between them and the ocean beyond. But back at the turn of the 19th century the same tidal system was put to more profitable use by the enterprising Langstone Gang, who ingeniously towed massive cargoes of contraband brandy in on submerged rafts at high tide, thus avoiding the attentions of any passing excise men, and carting them into the pub as soon as the waters subsided – by which time the offending vessel would be several miles out of sight.

Ye Olde Smugglers Inne [1358]

Although now known as *Ye Olde Smugglers Inne*, no-one would have dared refer to it as anything more sinister than *Market Cross Inn* in the days when it was owned by a villainous local butcher who led the ferocious Alfriston Gang of smugglers from the Sussex village of that name.

And today's visitors are left in no doubt of its colourful past by a massive fireplace surmounted by a thoroughly blood-curdling selection of swords and sundry instruments of torture

One of the oldest hostelries in the South-East, dating back to 1385 and with its brick floor polished by the feet of centuries, it began its lawless years considerably later than its William of Orange-inspired fellow privateers further west, taking advantage of the local military and police involvement with the Napoleonic Wars and consequent absence from local surveillance to launch its landlord's highly rewarding entry into the unlicensed trade.

At dead of night, columns of Collins' men would snake between pub and shoreline, passing the newly-arrived 'hot' cargo from hand to hand. When justice finally caught up with him, Collins was deported to Australia in 1831 – not for smuggling but for sheep-stealing...

At the same time a very similar trade was being carried out from the pub just up the road. But the big advantage enjoyed by the clientele of the *Star Inn* was the fact that it once belonged to the monks of Battle Abbey and contained a 'sanctuary post' that offered fugitives and smugglers instant church protection.

The post is there to this day – sadly stripped of its protective powers – at one corner of a cosy, low-beamed bar, whose servery is little more than a hole in the wall. And punters with a receptive facility for such manifestations can still be joined at the table by one such protected smuggler, the vociferous ghost of a 6' 5" gentleman with a smutty beard and top hat. And a trophy of one raid upon a stricken Dutch warship was its figurehead which has become a familiar Alfriston landmark on the pavement outside the pub – a grotesque red lion.

Further along the coast, up a wonderfully antique cobbled street in Rye, Russell Thorndyke used *The Mermaid* as the setting for his Dr Syn novels, involving a charismatic smuggling parson. The location was well-chosen because during the 18th century this was the headquarters of the vicious Hawkhurst gang, a ruthless band of smugglers whose grip on the neighbourhood was so terrifying that the law would not touch them and locals refused to testify against them for fear of their lives.

Today this splendid inn, dating back to 1156, offers no such discouragements to casual chat and richly deserves the accolade awarded to it by Leonard P Thompson in his celebrated volume, *Romantic Old Inns:* 'The Mermaid is unquestionably the most beautiful of all smugglers' inns and undoubtedly one of the loveliest of all the inns of England. It stands in Mermaid Street, for which thoroughfare it is claimed – and justly claimed – that no other street in the world exhibits such a wealth of antiquity; and of this antiquity the best specimen is the Mermaid Tavern.'

But not all villagers were built of such timid stock. The *Star and Eagle*, in Goudhurst, near Tunbridge Wells, with its wonderful commanding views over the orchards and hop fields of the Weald, was the strategically-sited 18th century headquarters of a gang of smugglers who terrorised the neighbourhood.

Eventually, the villagers turned out in force to fight a pitched battle with the villains and routed them – later having the satisfaction of witnessing the leader being hanged from a gibbet on nearby Horsmonden Heath.

Pubs have not always been the home of the quiet pint.

Chapter eighteen

Keeping things going

So what is the best chance that the British pub has of denying the doom merchants their final told-you-so and keeping a great British tradition alive into the centuries ahead?

One of the men to whom I was introduced on my first day on the *Manchester Evening News* was a curly-headed reporter called John Dodd.

The thing about Doddy, apart from the fact that he became an eloquent *Sun* feature writer and a towering – if somewhat ruffled – figure around Fleet Street was that, way back in 1938, he was born in a pub.

And what a pub! Nine years earlier, John's dad, Arthur Millington Dodd, took over the licence of the *Harrow* in Steep, Hampshire – can't miss it, go not to the little village of Steep but, just to confuse things, make for the neighbouring village of Sheet, cross the level crossing, go over the motorway, nip up the road a few hundred yards and look out for a narrow lane on the right before you get to Steep (if you get to Steep you've gone too far) – which stands today, if you can find it, totally unaltered by the passage of the years, a monumental time capsule in the evolution of the great British pub.

And now allow me yet another digression. We will, of course, return to the *Harrow* – for a very good reason – but while we are talking of pubs that have defied the temptation to follow the latest trend, if you happen to be in the West Country and are looking for a pub that looks and feels like the sort of pub that pubs always used to look and feel like, just try and find the *Crown Inn*. Again it's not easy. The clue is that it's in the village of Churchill, Somerset, up a little lane off the main road which isn't that easy to spot and it doesn't help that the sign seems to have fallen off the pub. Skinners Lane is what to look for but that probably isn't advertised either.

Back around 1985 Tim Rodgers returned to a beloved boozer in Bristol to discover it had been taken over and the beer was no longer dispensed direct from barrels behind the bar. Bemoaning this downward turn to the lady who was soon to become his wife, she said he ought to try a pint at her local, the *Crown* in Churchill.

Come the wedding day, Tim had an hour to kill before presenting himself at the altar rail. He wandered into the *Crown* for a livener. 'The owner told me that the pub was up for sale and did I want to buy it?' recalls Tim. 'I ended up saying yes twice in one day – and at least one of those decisions has stood the test of time!'

Ever since that fateful day, Tim has fought to keep everything as it always was, fires roaring through the winter, beer straight from the barrel, a couple of dark, tiny bars that positively exude welcome and character. And food – only at lunchtime, mark you – of the essentially homely category: sundry casseroles, cauliflower cheese, beef sandwiches, ploughman's, that sort of thing. Unmissable.

And while on the subject of time standing still and moving about 700 miles northwards, don't ever think of wandering into Speyside whisky territory without tracking down the unique *Fiddichside Inn*, just outside Craigallachie, home of the unrivalled Macallan distillery.

Scotland isn't famous for its pubs and I've enjoyed many a pint in this Brandie family stronghold, but let me quote from the Campaign for Real Ale's own words:

> *A marvellous rural survival; a tiny bar at the end of a cottage in a beautiful spot by a bridge over the River Fiddich. The pub has been in the owner's family for 88 years. The public bar measures about 10 x 15ft, with a panelled original counter running down the length of the room and leaving only half of the space for customers. There is not enough room for any tables, only bar stools and a couple of benches. The back gantry is a simple three-bay affair and*

there is half-height wooden panelling on the walls. Opposite the counter is a coal fire and there are antique William Younger's and Robert Younger's IPA mirrors. That's it - no carpets, no food, no fruit machines, no piped music, no TV, no children - absolute heaven for lovers of unspoilt pubs.

I couldn't have put it better.

Which brings us back to the *Harrow* and for the very good reason that when Arthur Millington Dodd died in 1959, his wife Annie took over the licence but her daughter, Ellen, who married Eddie McCutcheon, did most of the work on a daily basis, assuming the licence on Annie's death in the early 1980s and on Ellen's death in 2004 it passed into the hands of their daughters, Claire and Nisa McCutcheon.

So the three times winner of the *Good Pub Guide's* Unspoilt Pub of the Year award has been in the same family's loving and protective care for not that far short of a century.

Over the years its regulars have included Lionel 'Bobby' Birch, who became Mandrake of the *Sunday Telegraph* and achieved the remarkable record of being seven times married, a dog who smoked a pipe, a local poacher who kept his 12-bore tied to his bicycle crossbar, the occasional shipload of Free French sailors and Jack Harris, better known as the *Day of the Triffids* writer, John Wyndham.

('The dog's name was Floss, a liver and white cocker spaniel,' recalls John. 'She sat in the corner with her owner Bill Greenaway, a brickie, and sometimes Bill would give her his pipe to smoke and say 'Draw, Floss, draw,' and Floss's cheeks would puff out and smoke would come out of her mouth. She never coughed.')

So honourably resistant to physical redesign, what better yardstick could there be from which to measure the changing daily life within the Great British Pub since the carefree pre-war days of the flappers and the Charleston?

John stared into his pint glass, as though searching for a vision of his earliest memories towards the end of World War Two. 'We didn't sell any food in those early days and I remember when we got our first potato crisps – the word got around and in no time there was a queue outside the door,' said John.

'And there were regular beer shortages. My father used to run out from time to time but was totally unrepentant. He would simply post one of his famous ditties on the board outside. 'My bottles are empty, my barrels are dry – I'm off to the seaside, ta ta, goodbye' was one that sticks in the mind.

'Every year my brother and I would build a bonfire across the road and make a Guy which would be left slumped in a chair against the pub wall. My dad, being a prankster, would occasionally remove the guy and replace it with himself. In the gloom of a November evening Jim the poacher would park his bike next to it, slump on the bench smoking his pipe waiting for the pub to open, whereupon my father would spring up, poke him in the eye and say "boo!"

'Our regular customers in those days were the local roadmen, gardeners, farm labourers, tractor drivers and teachers from nearby Bedales School, who used to regard the Harrow as their common room. And on Sunday mornings, of course, all the locals would have been out ferreting. So they came in for a game of darts carrying their nets with the ferrets in their pockets.

'Unusually for country pubs of that era, there were always one or two ladies in the bar, especially when Bobby Birch was in his pomp, and there would be more for the regular Saturday night sing-songs when we used to have a piano in the "second" bar played brilliantly by Flora Crane. The highlight came whenever Jim the poacher performed *McNamara's Band* with a chip tin lid hitting everyone on top of the head with it as he sang "and the drums go bang" (bonk went the chip tin lid on someone's head) "and the cymbals clang" (clonk went the chip tin lid on another head) – until he hit 'Funny Sid' with it and there was a full scale chip tin lid fight between two old men. One or two of the women played darts.

'Money was hard to come by. The mark-up we were allowed to charge was one old penny per pint so you had to sell twelve pints before you made a shilling. And if someone had no money he used to pay with rabbits. The going price for a rabbit was eleven pence, so my dad would give him a pint and that would be our lunch.

'And the toilet was across the road...'

'Which it still is,' interjected Claire McCutcheon, who nowadays runs the front of house while her sister, Nisa, produces her famous soups and marvellous comfort food in the kitchen.

'Back in the 1970s they tried to make us bring it inside but it would have ruined the place. Fortunately, the appropriate district council committee was chaired by a local dairy farmer, who was a friend of ours, and we got up a massive petition. It was the highest number of objections the local planning office had ever had and, in the end we won the day so that's another thing about the Harrow that has never changed.'

So you run across the road for a pee, no big deal.

'We were not entirely victorious in the toilets war,' John admits, 'because in those days the servery area was hung with hocks of ham in their netting, sucking up still more smoke from the Harrow pipe and ciggy puffers. God knows how this can have made them a health hazard because the ham was already smoked. But we had to concede that to the council so now they're kept in fridges.'

Claire continues the evolutionary tale: 'The first proper food we served was bread and cheese in 1959 or 1960 and over the years came soup, ploughman's lunch, scotch eggs and home-cooked ham or cheese and chutney sandwiches.

'Now we list everything that Nisa has prepared on squares of paper pinned to the wall – today, as you can see, there are rare beef sandwiches, egg mayonnaise sandwiches, Nisa's home-made flan quiche, treacle tart, nut-free chocolate biscuit crunch and, of course, pea and ham soup.'

And does the money now roll in? 'We have our 6 o'clock club – the regulars who come every evening, have two or three pints and go home about 7.30,' says Claire. 'At weekends the walkers turn up and usually sit outside during the summer. We're never going to get rich. But the Harrow is a tradition and it's well worth keeping it going. It ticks over quite nicely.'

It does more than that. On the day I popped in recently, both bars were crammed; there were folk at the tables outside and scarcely enough room for John's dog and mine to have a half way decent barking match.

The *Harrow*, the *Crown Inn* and the *Fiddichside Inn* are living proof that as far as the Great British Pub is concerned, the more things *don't* change, the better its chance of survival. Forget the gastro menus, the fancy cocktails, the giant TV screens; the old ones might still be the best.

Let us drink to the 21st century – and a third millennium in which someone somewhere is forever insisting 'It's my round.'

INDEX OF PUBS

Lightning Source UK Ltd.
Milton Keynes UK
UKOW021200030212

186596UK00002B/75/P